LITERALLY
VIRTUALLY

MAKING VIRTUAL TEAMS WORK
-REVISED AND EXPANDED EDITION-

Featuring the latest research on
telecommuting trends,
hybrid team effectiveness
and the Long-Distance Leadership Model™

LEE S. JOHNSEN, CPT, CPLP, SPHR

Child of the Prairie Press
Madison, Wisconsin

Contents

To the workplace pioneers
who acknowledge that rich potential
comes from diversity of thought, word and deed

Foreword

Over the past 35 years I have had the privilege of starting four companies. This would not have been possible without the dedicated help and support of some fantastic leaders and teams of individual contributors. Early in my career, I also worked for a number of large corporations, government agencies and other entrepreneurial startups.

During this time span I've seen the behaviors and practices of employees evolve dramatically. These changes have been driven by a number of social, political, and technological factors. It's obvious that today's workforce is more mobile, and less traditional. New technologies for virtual communication and meetings have allowed us to do things that we could only dream of when I started my career decades ago. But with each of these advances, I've also seen new challenges arise.

When I talk to leaders today, I often hear questions like, "How can I manage a team that I may never meet face-to-face? How do I keep my employees informed and engaged when they can't participate in casual lunchroom or water cooler conversations? How do I spot early signs of performance-related issues before they go too far or get overwhelming? How can I create a sense of cooperation and team spirit among people who work remotely? How can I attract and engage the next generation of team members, and retain the valuable ones I already have?" Interestingly, these types of questions come from all levels of leadership and all types of organizations.

Unfortunately, I had to learn how to manage remote teams and employees the hard way when building my first companies. Through trial and error, I would experiment with a variety of techniques. For example, in one of my companies, I had three software development teams, one in Poland, one in India, and one in the United States. I also had contracted developers and software engineers in every time zone in North America. One reason we did this was to create a 24/7 software development cycle where "the sun would never set" on our programming and quality assurance resources. While one team was sleeping, one would be coding and the final one would be testing. This also allowed us to rapidly respond to the demands of our global customers for the latest and most innovative features. However, the challenge of dealing with these various remote teams with different time zones, languages, and cultures was daunting.

Lee Johnsen has spent his career helping people in organizations learn, grow, and solve difficult problems like these. He has done this with very practical and easy-to- follow advice. This new edition of his book tackles many of these challenging issues with a convenient model that provides a detailed blueprint about how to build, motivate, and lead remote teams. What I find most useful about this book is that Lee has done significant research and testing to help readers bypass most of the costly mistakes I made through my trial and error process.

As a training and development professional, I also appreciate that this book is designed as both a personal development guide and a team-training tool. So, if you lead a remote team or anticipate that you might want to train your team, this book can help on both levels. Lee has also supplied a number of tools in the book, including discussion questions, checklists, visual models, and assessments. He even has scripts of conversations, so that readers can visualize actual remote team interactions.

I wish I'd had a book like this when I started building and working with my remote teams. I know we could have saved a lot of time and money by not having to learn from costly mistakes.

But now, you can access this wealth of information without having to search through Google or YouTube. As team members and organizations continue to be impacted by technology, I believe this book will become even more valuable over time. I would definitely put this book on the "mandatory reading list" for all leaders, regardless of organization type or size.

Frank Russell
CEO, Prositions, Inc.

Introduction

The path of the past that leads us to the present and future is a curious one. The extent to which that path is the result of intention or chance or both is unknown. While we may like to think it is primarily by intention that we find ourselves in our current circumstances, I believe there are likely equal doses of one's spirit and mystery.

I grew up in a rural community in the middle of eastern South Dakota. My parents were farmers and ranchers. We were brought up with the notion that work came first and if, by some small chance, we found ourselves with a little free time, it was best not to admit it (lest we hear from one of our parents, "I'll find something else for you to do").

I also come from an extended family of teachers. Before she married my father, my mother was a teacher. Her two brothers were teachers, as was her mother. I suppose some of that couldn't help but rub off on me. As a second grader, I recall trying to help one of my classmates learn to read.

My parents had an interest in different cultures and people in other parts of the world and they often opened our home to guests from other countries. The first was a man from Panama who stayed with us for three weeks. It was the first time I'd ever met a person of color. Other guests followed from Japan, Switzerland and Germany.

After graduating from college, my first job was to work for the U.S. Department of Agriculture (USDA) Cooperative Extension Service as a 4-H and Youth Leader in Iowa. Our mission was to be a resource and guide to helping young people become productive, contributing citizens. I'd like to think I contributed to that mission in some small way. In teaching youth, I think I learned as much (probably more) as my participants.

My next job was in another branch of USDA as a colleague of employees responsible for making agricultural and rural housing loans to low income rural families. This was during a particularly tumultuous time referred to as the 1980s Farm Crisis. For the first time in the Iowa agency, my boss and State Director, Robert Pimm, recognized that while we had a staff who were highly skilled in the technical aspects of lending, they lacked sufficient interpersonal skills to help farm families deal with the emotionally charged decisions one must make when faced with financial calamity.

Part of my job was to plan and coordinate employee training and we began to balance the focus of the technical aspects of finance with the interpersonal skills of listening, empathy, communications skills and teamwork. From that point on, I was hooked. My career path led me to the field of learning and development and performance improvement in various roles in three different organizations. It felt like a good match (and still does).

As I entered what I thought at the time was the midpoint of my life and career, I found myself wanting to recalibrate and figure out a new direction. I had just ended a marriage and the organizational culture within my workplace was not healthy. These factors were taking a toll on me, so this self-imposed time of reflection prompted me to examine what was truly and personally important to me and how I could best be an agent for making a positive difference.

I challenged myself to write a personal mission statement, life goals and what became my "Personal Leadership Credo" which consisted of the Top 10 List of Leadership Practices. The common theme among these was to "improve human performance in the world." It was then that I decided to chart a path for a leap into entrepreneurship and to create my consulting firm, Partners in Development.

Partners in Development represents my mission and goals of "improving human performance in the world." Since 2002, my life's work has been about "closing gaps in workplace performance." I have had the privilege of speaking at international conferences on the topic of Long-Distance Leadership for virtual teams and the remote workforce. In 2014, I spent five months working with young leaders in Saudi Arabia and have taught various groups about leadership around the globe. It is through these associations that I became fascinated by the differences between on-site teams and those in the virtual workforce who are separated by physical distance, time zones, technology and most importantly, different cultures. Through my research and practical experience of both working virtually and leading virtual teams, I've learned that organizations and teams that do not recognize and address these differences risk disappointing results and low employee engagement.

I knew I could help change that.

I've written this book because virtual teams and the remote workforce are no longer a way of the future, they are the way of today. More and more, all businesses from small startup companies to large global organizations are relying on the benefits and talents of a workforce not constrained by location. But these benefits do not come without a price. Leaders and team members who work virtually, even part of the time, must learn to communicate and collaborate differently than onsite teams. Research has shown that there are important differences between these two team types and unless they are planned for and addressed, performance results will be sacrificed.[1]

For the past several years, I have dedicated my life's work to discovering the key differences that lead to success for remote workers and virtual teams. Knowing those differences has led me to create a model and a process for high performance. To support the model, I have created tools, techniques, assessments and trainings to address these differences. This book represents a compilation of many of them. There are many more to be discovered and I look forward to sharing these with you in the future.

For this book, I completed an industry-wide survey of over 500 employees working as member and leaders of virtual teams across the world. The findings of my research are listed in callout boxes throughout this book, and some of the statistics may shock you, such as the one below:

Did You Know?
Over 76% of national and international employees have clear business needs to work virtually.

We are all remote workers. Who today doesn't use technology to communicate with our families and coworkers? We email, text, leave voice messages, video conference with friends, children and grandchildren and participate in social media to both share and receive news from those who are important to us.

I wrote this book because, even though we leverage the power of virtual communication, we often default to doing so as if we are always face-to-face. There's a difference. This book is filled with best practices to help you and your virtual workforce members not only survive, but to excel. To quote a colleague, "We need to work together as if we're all in the same room, although we're not.[2] It is my hope that every reader of this book will find ways to create a greater sense of working in the same room, even if you're not.

CHAPTER 1

The Planning Meeting

"What have I gotten myself into?" It all began on Thursday morning. This was to be the first day that Shonda's entire virtual team had the opportunity to meet in person.

Shonda was tapped by Karl Norris, Chief Marketing Officer, in the first quarter of the year to lead a new task force at EMCA Foodservice. The goal of the task force was to draft a dynamite business development plan to globally expand their foodservice company.

Currently, EMCA Foodservice, Inc. operates in the U.S., with access to a few suppliers in Brazil. However, there appears to be a great opportunity to expand into other global markets, specifically China, Greece and Saudi Arabia. Shonda was elated as Karl discussed the project and placed her in charge of building a multinational task force from within EMCA Foodservice, preferably one comprised of employees that represented the target countries being considered for business expansion.

Shonda knew if she did well with this assignment, her promotion to Vice President of Marketing would be a sure thing. Now, as her task force argued around the conference table, she wasn't so sure.

THE TEAM

Six weeks after speaking with Karl, Shonda assembled her team. The team includes:

- **Jeff** was Shonda's pick as a project manager. With Shonda as the team lead, she needed a dependable and energetic person to help scope out tasks, assignments and deliverables and to administer timelines for the task force.
- **Vasili** is an expert in business development and sales. He has been with the company for 25 years, mostly in the U.S., but returned to his birthplace of Athens, Greece for two years to begin exploring potential markets and develop relationships with local government contacts and suppliers.

- **Liling** is one of two strategists on the team. After growing up in China, Liling, she came to the U.S. where she received her bachelor's degree in finance and her MBA with an emphasis in international business. She now lives in Beijing and, like Vasili, has been tracking EMCA Foodservice's competition in China and the risks of expanding into additional markets.
- **Hamad**, the second strategist, joined the company only a few weeks before he was tapped to join Shonda's team. In addition to his IT expertise, Hamad previously worked for a large restaurant chain in Saudi Arabia and understands how the foodservice business in his country operates and the requirements needed to gain their government's approval.
- **Gustavo** is located in Sao Paulo, Brazil and has been tracking the performance of six EMCA Foodservice products already in Brazil and strongly believes the market in Brazil offers room to debut additional products. In addition to his business development background, he has used customer analytics to anticipate customer demand and increase sales 200% over the past three years in Brazil.

- The last person to join the team is **Aisha**, who is located in Mumbai, India. Aisha is an expert in international finance and business analytics and came to EMCA Foodservice with strong recommendations from her previous employer. She is an independent contractor who was originally filling in for a financial analyst on maternity leave. She proved to be invaluable to the Finance department, so her contract was extended, but she has yet to receive a full-time offer.
- **Shonda** is a 10-year veteran at EMCA Foodservice, and has worked as a project manager and strategist before moving into Marketing. A native of New York, Shonda is a mover and shaker and is well-respected by EMCA Foodservice's executive team.

With this team of intelligent, successful and driven professionals, Shonda expected nothing but success as they began meeting virtually to create their strategy and steps for execution. Six months later, she was excited to meet the entire team in person in Chicago, but she didn't expect the conflict she was now seeing before her eyes.

THE MEETING

The team members were excited to finally meet face-to-face to prepare for their big presentation to senior management on Monday morning. The plan was for everyone to meet in Chicago on Thursday at 10 AM. That would give them most of Thursday and Friday to prepare and be ready.

Though Friday is not typically a work day for Hamad (due to his Arabic heritage), he had reluctantly agreed on the condition that he would be allowed time away for prayer. Unfortunately, due to flight delays, Liling, Vasili and Aisha arrived late to Chicago. Now at 2:00 in the afternoon, the team members were all finally assembled in a conference room, some suffering from jet lag, some annoyed by the four-hour delay and all anxious to start the meeting.

Because they were already behind schedule, Shonda decided to get down to business right away.

SHONDA: Alright everyone, let's get started. You should all have received the revised agenda this morning via email, and...

JEFF: Shonda, don't you think we should have some face time with each other before jumping into the agenda? You know, do an icebreaker or something?

GUSTAVO: Great idea! Let's start off with "Two Truths and a Lie"! I am so good at this game because I enjoy poker, and I can keep a straight face. See, I'll demonstrate...

JEFF: As much as I'm sure everyone appreciates your enthusiasm, Gustavo, let's opt for something more professional.

SHONDA: We'll have plenty of time after we wrap business today to chat and get to know each other, but we're behind schedule today. So, as I was saying, let's...

HAMAD: I didn't receive the agenda.

AISHA: (scoots chair closer to him) Hamad, I can share with you on my laptop.

HAMAD: (looks alarmed and leans away) No, I just want to begin. (speaks quieter) And, I now see the agenda in my email. Continue.

SHONDA: (takes a deep breath before continuing) I'd like to thank you all for your hard work so far. This is a major undertaking and all of your contributions to date are valued.

VASILI: Well, if you want to get something done, everyone knows I'm the strongest link. I'm connected to everyone in the industry and EMCA Foodservice brought me back because they knew they couldn't run this ship without me!

LILING: (under her breath) Then why did they fire you in the first place?

Jeff snickers, and Vasili's face turns red and he flashes a stern look at Liling.

VASILI: (to Liling) Once you're finished with your *internship*, you should be so lucky to work for a company for almost 20 years.

LILING: Intern? I have an MBA!

GUSTAVO: Hey guys, no need to argue! In Brazil, we have a saying, "Estou feito ao bife!", which means "we don't have a problem"...although in English, I think it translates to "we are done to the beef"...hmmm, that doesn't make much sense, now does it?

JEFF: Guys, we should really get focused here. I personally would like Liling and Hamad to give an overview of the strategy you were both responsible for.

SHONDA: I'm sorry, Jeff, but I believe I was leading this meeting.

VASILI: Does it matter who leads the meeting? I mean, I have the most tenure here. Maybe I should lead the meeting!

SHONDA: (ignoring Vasili) I would like to suggest that since we are getting such a late start today due to travel delays, we are going to need to work through the weekend. If we can complete the groundwork for this presentation by Friday, we can relax a little on Saturday and reconvene on Sunday afternoon to rehearse the presentation and make sure we're completely ready to deliver our findings to senior leadership.

(the room erupts into sounds of protest and displeasure at Shonda's suggestion)

JEFF: Well, I, for one, cannot make it on Sunday. It's my son's fourth birthday. I cannot leave Terrance alone to handle the decorations; he gets way too stressed.

SHONDA: Well, I planned on attending First Sunday at church, but sometimes sacrifices have to be made.

HAMAD: Yes, I feel if I am being forced to work on Friday, my day of prayer, then everyone else can work on their day of prayer, as well. It's only fair.

VASILI: Listen everyone, I say we just table this conversation for now and see how much we get done today.

SHONDA: Agreed. Ok, Liling and Hamad, can we begin with the strategy overview?

JEFF: (rolls his eyes and grumbles) I already said that...

LILING: Well, I can present to you what I did. HAMAD never sent his slides to me after I asked for them *three times*, so...

HAMAD: (to Liling) I didn't agree with your initial approach to the strategy, so I was waiting to see what you prepared first before showing you my findings. After all, the goal is to expand into Saudi Arabia, *followed* by China, then Greece.

LILING: (turns to Hamad) No, the goal is to start with China, then Greece and finally Saudi Arabia!

HAMAD: (to Liling) I think you may be confused. (turns to Aisha) And, Aisha's financial projections seemed too low. I found many discrepancies in her report, so I think she should go first and explain her findings.

(Aisha looks up quickly and is embarrassed)

SHONDA: Yes, I also thought those numbers were a little low. Good eye, Hamad.

AISHA: (to the group) If I may, what numbers are we talking about? I'm unclear about the country we are focusing on right now.

SHONDA: (frustrated to Aisha) I mentioned last week to pull together projections on our secondary markets. That would be Brazil and Saudi Arabia. Did you get my text?

AISHA: I thought Brazil was a primary market and Greece was secondary because Vasili was already there working on sales channels and the other countries were going to be analyzed in Phase 2. At least, that's what this document from our meeting two weeks ago said...

SHONDA: Did anyone else believe we were waiting to look at Saudi Arabia and China in Phase 2?

VASILI, JEFF and LILING: (all begin shouting differing views)

HAMAD: (passes a stack of documents around table) I revised the projections for Saudi Arabia, and I think it would be best to go with these numbers, and it shows why my country should also be in Phase 1.

Aisha fights to be heard over the disagreeing crowd as Gustavo interrupts.

GUSTAVO: (smiles triumphantly) Well, I have been working on expanding our potential in Brazil and – (slams hand loudly on table) – I think that is the best place to start operations! (animatedly) Let me paint the picture for you...we start off by...

VASILI: (to Gustavo) You know, excitement doesn't equal sales, though. I remember when I was doing your job many moons ago, our partners valued my professionalism! You think you can just cha cha your way into these meetings and take over? It takes years of experience and building a network to...

Shonda looks around the room disappointedly knowing that they are far from ready to present to upper management. It is painfully obvious they are not on the same page, and she suddenly realizes she has not been an effective team leader.

"What have I gotten myself into?"

CHAPTER 2

The Keys to Virtual Team Success

What Shonda and her team members soon realized in their first face-to-face meeting was that things had not been going well for some time. Various differences and conflicts within the team had laid below the surface in the interest in getting through the tasks. Though quite successful in their individual achievements and their ability to work onsite within their countries, the experience of working virtually was different. The large differences in time zones, geography, culture and technology made their work more complex and time consuming. How did Shonda miss these cues?

While Shonda is a skilled leader, she was so focused on getting the work done, that she had neglected some of the unique elements necessary to lead a global virtual team. Without a full understanding of how these differences affect the team's work, it is unlikely to guarantee the team's success.

> ### Did You Know?
> 34% of employees believe their team leader does not have the right skills the team needs.

In 2014, the Business Research Consortium published a report titled The *New Dominance of Virtual Team and Leaders* that illustrates how virtual teams are different from other teams in several ways.[3] In a study of over 1,500 virtual team members and leaders, they found the following to be most important:

- Team communication - 70%
- Better listening - 63%
- Building trust - 50%
- Explicit goal setting - 45%
- Establishing processes - 42%
- Checkpoints - 42%

It is not uncommon to assume that leading a virtual team is similar to leading a team of co- located members. In the same research mentioned above, nearly 60% of respondents said that first-level managers are "mediocre" or "worse" as virtual leaders. The numbers are only slightly less for middle managing leaders. Moreover, leaders of global virtual teams face the greatest challenges. In addition to the challenges previously mentioned, global virtual teams often have team members who are inexperienced working virtually and have less training about how to work in virtual teams. As in Shonda's team, there is often greater reliance among team members' goals and there is not always equal access to various types for communication technologies.

Did You Know?
41% of U.S. employees work in a virtual team and DO NOT work on-site in their organization.

Unfortunately, Shonda and her team didn't fully recognize these differences and now they were paying the price. What could they have done differently? In the remaining sections of this book we'll look deeper into a model for virtual team success and specific strategies and methods for creating high virtual team performance. For now, let's start with an overview.

The Long-Distance Leadership Model for High-Performing Virtual Teams (aka Making Virtual Teams Work)

In the years I have worked with virtual teams and their organizations, I have come to understand some very real differences faced by virtual team leaders and their members — including their struggles and what leads to their success. Based on my experiences, I developed a framework of fundamental phases all successful teams go through. This is called the **Long-Distance Leadership Model™ for High-Performing Virtual Teams.**

PLAN – Why are we here?

Plan represents the thinking and work that must be done before the team is assembled. It consists of gaining an understanding of the critical elements that lay the groundwork for success. In this stage, the following questions should yield answers that reveal important information about your prospective team:

- What are the organizational factors that are driving the need for this team? Why is a virtual team the best option to meet the organization's need?
- What are potential obstacles that could impact the team's ability to accomplish its purpose (e.g. access to information, multiple reporting relationships, and differences in culture, time, geography, and technology, etc.)?
- What resources will be required?
- What are the team's purpose and expected results, and what does success look like?
- Which team leader and team member skills are required to achieve the desired results?

Without answering these questions, virtual teams are likely to struggle and potentially fail before they have the initial meeting. Key stakeholders must be involved and agree on these lest the team not achieve those intended results.

PREPARE – How should we work?

Once the initial plan has been described, the next phase is to move to **Prepare** by identifying and selecting the team members who either have the required technical and virtual skills or who are willing and able to develop them. In many virtual teams, members come from different technical backgrounds and functions. They are likely to be highly skilled in fields such as marketing, finance, sales, operations, or human resources. Yet, while crucial to the team's success, it is the unique skills related to virtual teams that are often more challenging. Building rapid trust, leveraging technology, self-awareness and self-management, relationship management, and virtual communication are essential to team success.

Once members have been selected, it's important to properly onboard the team around its purpose, vision and goals. This also includes creating agreements as to how they will communicate, collaborate, make decisions, and share information. Only after these elements are completed is the team ready to launch into their work. Without these, there will be confusion, conflicts and missed opportunities, with team progress being compromised as a consequence.

> ### Did You Know?
> *19% of employees are on a team without a clear vision and mission.*

PRODUCE – What moves us forward?

After the team has launched, the real work begins — it is time to **Produce** results. This is the most active phase and the most vulnerable stage for things to go wrong. As team members go about accomplishing their individual tasks there are likely to be situations that don't go as expected. Regardless of their members' technical skills, all teams encounter challenges. For teams like Shonda's, where the work produced by one or more team members can have a significant influence on the outputs of other members, breakdowns in communication, trust, and collaboration can cause a ripple effect that can be disastrous. Members of High Complexity/High Reliance global virtual teams must build trusting relationships, be able to track and assess their performance and be incentivized to achieve their intended goals. We will discuss more about Complexity and Reliance for virtual teams in Chapter 3. In many cases, mobile workers report directly to someone other than their team leader and are not devoted full-time to their virtual team. These team leaders soon learn that they must build trusting, collaborative relationships with the direct managers of their team members, as well. What could Shonda have done to navigate the challenges associated with this phase of her team's work?

RESULTS – When do we shine?

As team members begin to achieve milestones and they demonstrate **Results,** the behaviors of highly-effective team membership, excitement often builds. This is where their hard work up front begins to pay off and they experience "flow", where they are both productive and having fun. As one goal after another is completed, the team celebrates both the milestones and the final results. The energy becomes contagious and members are exhilarated despite their hard work.

Did You Know?

45% of employees say their team does NOT use a tool or system to track milestones.

REVIEW, ADJUST, REDIRECT – What did we miss?

For teams that are successful, this phase is a real source of learning at the end of a temporary team's work, such as a task force or a committee. For on-going virtual teams, a periodic "look back" can be a source of insight and inspiration. When members make time to reflect, they gain a deeper understanding of the practices and behaviors that worked well and what could be done differently in future teams. By sharing these learnings with others, the organization becomes all the stronger as a player in the virtual world.

However, not every team's journey to performance is a smooth one.

Many virtual teams struggle to reach 'flow.' During those struggles, it becomes crucial to loop back to identify what is not working well and what adjustments are needed to get back on track. This may require an adjustment to the Team Operating Agreement (more on this later) or redirecting members to the agreements made, but not being followed.

A good rule of thumb is to **Review** the status of your team at each stage before moving to the next section. For example, if a virtual team is about to move into the Prepare stage without having identified the team vision, it is best to **Adjust** the agenda to solidify a vision and then, **Redirect** the group to continue on.

Had Shonda and her team known and practiced the steps within each phase of the Long-Distance Leadership Model, they would likely be experiencing a very different situation than their current one.

What Makes Virtual Teams Work: Eight Predictors of High Performance

Over the years, as virtual teams and the mobile workforce have become more commonplace, some significant research into the differences between them and the dynamics of co-located teams has emerged. This research has led to some powerful insights into these differences and now provides guidance to not only predict high performance, but how to plan, prepare and produce it.

In this section, I will distill the most relevant research and offer insights into what those eight predictors for high-performing teams are and how you can identify them.

PLAN

1. Articulate team purpose and vision

There are five areas that should be addressed at the onset of a virtual team: 1) team purpose and vision, 2) environment, 3) team description, 4) team membership and 5) the team agreements.

Team Purpose and Vision: the first predictor of high performance is the extent to which virtual team members have a clear and shared sense of purpose (who we are and what we deliver) and vision (what will result if we are wildly successful). The purpose and vision connect the virtual team to the larger organization and provide a clear sense of direction and alignment.

Environment: the environment identifies the organizational drivers behind the need for the team to operate virtually (versus an onsite team) and invites a realistic assessment of potential obstacles and resources required for the team's success before it is launched.

Team Description: this statement provides a sense of team identity (name), determines goals and provides a scope of the team's work. It considers the team member skills necessary to accomplish those goals. And, if this is a temporary versus an ongoing virtual team, the description defines the intended duration of the team based on its goals.

Team Membership: Successful virtual team members have a balance of technical and interpersonal skills. Once the required technical skills have been identified, emotional intelligence skills of self-awareness and self-management, awareness of the feelings of others and relationship management are essential to healthy productive teamwork.

> ### Did You Know?
> *11% of U.S. employees do NOT have a favorable relationship with their team members.*

Investing time to articulate and document these elements is a proactive approach to garnering understanding and alignment among team members and with stakeholders outside the team. If there are differences in interpretations, they can be discussed and worked out earlier rather than later.

2. Determine skills needed for overall team

In the first quarter of 2010, the Society for Human Resource Management (SHRM) Research Quarterly stated, "Effective leadership is the number one factor that influences success in a virtual organization."[4] There is a correlation between the extent to which organizations say they have good virtual leaders and the degree to which they see virtual leaders and leaders of collocated work groups as different. This influences everything from leadership development strategies to specific tactics for meeting facilitation.

Compared to leaders of collocated workgroups, leaders of high performing virtual teams are more effective at:

- Empowering team members
- Ensuring that the job gets done
- Emphasizing collective mission/purpose
- Considering varying levels/skills of team members
- Articulating a vision
- Coordinating various business functions[5]

Did You Know?
19% of employees are on a team
without a clear vision and mission.

What makes leaders of virtual teams more effective? The secret is they have learned to adapt to the differences of geography, time, technology and culture. For instance, they have learned to build rapid trust with team members they rarely see face-to-face. They become much more explicit in their communication and have learned to provide feedback and coach with respect to cultural differences among their team members. These are some of the key skills highly associated with emotional intelligence.

> ### *Did You Know?*
> *35% of employees are NOT comfortable communicating that they feel disrespected or insulted by a team member or team leader.*

Had Shonda understood these differences, she likely would have invested time applying these techniques to her team and thus averting some of the problems she is facing. But Shonda is not alone. In a 2013 joint study conducted by the Canadian Management Centre (CMC), American Management Association (AMA) and the Management Centre Europe (MCE), nearly 1,200 participants delivered feedback on the topic of virtual team leadership. Their responses revealed that nearly 67% believe that virtual teams in their organizations suffer from poor leadership. In addition, 'inconsistent" or "inappropriate" leadership was seen as a serious impediment to successful teams. **Clearly, effective leadership is a challenge for virtual teams.** A leadership effectiveness assessment tool can be an important resource to identifying the strengths and development needs of virtual team leaders and guide focused development actions. A sample of our Virtual Team Leader Self-Assessment is in my online resource center at **LiterallyVirtually.com.**

Here are a few best practices for highly-effective virtual team leaders to adopt:

- **Allow more time for virtual team members to communicate with one another** - not only is the communication about tasks, schedules, work processes, and procedures. They also need to allow time to build relationships. The highest performing teams develop strong, trusting bonds among their members. These members share interests beyond work tasks and include the kind of social bonding that occurs around the proverbial water cooler or lunchroom.
- **Leverage technology** - team leaders who learn to leverage the communications and collaboration technology available to them are more likely to gain and maintain team member engagement. They also match the technology methods to the messages they want to communicate. They pick and choose the technology that is most likely to facilitate communication. They're selective about using email and text. When topics are likely to become emotional, they choose technology that has a visual component so that they can get a better sense of nonverbal responses that are such an important part of communication.

- **Be specific** – there is a saying among virtual team leaders, "Anything that can go wrong with a face-to-face team, can go wrong with a virtual team, only usually faster and less gracefully." Virtual team leaders and members need to learn to be very specific in their communication and to check frequently to ensure the same understanding.

Did You Know?
49% of employees have a team leader
that does NOT ask for input to gauge all
members' moods and thoughts.

PREPARE

3. Select and onboard team members

What sets highly effective virtual team members apart are not their technical skills or IQ. Certainly, technical skills are important, but the real differentiator is their emotional intelligence. There is abundant research that emotional intelligence is the key differentiator between average and high performing individuals. According to Travis Bradberry, noted emotional intelligence expert, research conducted by TalentSmart compared emotional intelligence (EQ) with 33 other important workplace skills, and found that emotional intelligence is the strongest predictor of performance, explaining a full 58% of success in all types of jobs. He goes on to note that 90% of top performers are also high in emotional intelligence. These findings hold true for people in all industries, at all levels, in every region of the world. Not only that, but both performance and salary are tied closely to emotional intelligence.[6]

When selecting virtual team members, the emotional intelligence skills of self-awareness, self-management, social awareness, and relationship management are strongly weighted. Communicating virtually is naturally more complex and more time consuming. While advances in technology have certainly enhanced our ability to connect and collaborate, they still can't match the face-to-face communication experience. Virtual team members and leaders must adapt in order to build strong and trusting relationships across boundaries.

Additional team member skills such as project management, communications technology

(which we will discuss shortly) and organizational skills are also important for the success of a virtual team. If not already present among team members, these skills can usually be developed as needed. An assessment tool that measures the strengths and development needs of virtual team members can also guide focused development. A sample of our Virtual Team Member Self-Assessment can be found in my online resource center at **LiterallyVirtually.com**.

The other good news is that, unlike IQ (which is established early in life), EQ can develop and continue to grow throughout our lifetime. Strong virtual team members communicate with teammates, commit and follow through and collaborate to achieve results.

4. Create clear agreements

Have you ever made a terrible mistake despite having the best intentions? This happened to James, an American virtual team leader who was leading a project team made up of members from the U.S. and other countries across the globe, including Su Min from Japan. Su Min had done an outstanding job in accomplishing her tasks for the team and had gone above and beyond in helping other team members with their parts.

James wanted to recognize Su Min for her contributions to the team. One day during a team meeting, he pointed out all of Su Min's accomplishments and praised her for all that she had done to help the team. Su Min said nothing. "Why was Su Min silent?" James thought to himself. "I thought she'd be pleased."

Later that day, James received a call from Su Min's direct manager in Japan. He was told that Su Min had resigned. What happened? Sun Min felt she had been humiliated in front of the team and could no longer be effective. In her culture, it is not appropriate to single out an individual from the team; the group is more important than any individual.

How could James have avoided this terrible error? James' lack of awareness and understanding of cultural differences including Su Min's preference for private recognition, resulted in very different consequences from what he expected. What he received, instead, was the unintended result of a well-intended action.

Clear agreements about how virtual team leaders and their members will communicate and collaborate to achieve their shared purpose and vision is an essential ingredient to high performance. Often described and documented as a Team Operating Agreement (TOA) or Team Charter, the agreement is ideally a part of the onboarding process for a newly formed team.

While every Team Operating Agreement is unique and should be adapted to meet specific needs of the team, there are some key elements commonly found in them. Your team may not need to use them all, but components common to most virtual team operating agreements are shown in the example here:

Team Operating Agreement Elements

- Team Name and Description
- Team Purpose, Vision and Goals
- Team Leader and Member Skills Required
- Resources and Support (available to the team)
- Potential Barriers (that could impact the team's ability to succeed)
- Team Communication and Collaboration Protocols (how they will work together)
  - Level of participation expected
  - Communications Technology the team will use and timeliness of responses from team member requests
  - Team Meeting Practices
  - Team Member Communication Preferences and Styles
  - Decision Making Approaches
  - Conflict Resolution Steps

Team Communication and Collaboration Protocols serve as the guidelines and ground rules to help the team work together most productively. These can be formal or informal. Geographic, ethnic and cultural differences impact how effectively individuals collaborate and teams operate. Awareness of these differences is vital if communications are to be clear, honest and properly directed. **This is a "living document" and should be updated throughout the duration of the team's engagement.**

Developing a communications agreement can open discussion about several work process factors critical to the team's success and enables team members to get to know one another, build trust, identify differences and collaborate. Creating this agreement early in the team's development can clarify expectations and reduce conflicts when team members commit to it and hold one another accountable for their agreements.

For existing or ongoing teams, the TOA can serve as a tool to build alignment to the team's purpose, vision and goals. This agreement can also serve as a checkpoint for members who have been working together for a while. Finally, it can assist the members to identify strengths, areas of improvement and any changes needed.

Whether your team is just forming or if its members have been together for a while, one principle holds true - **never assume everyone has the same understanding of the components of the team operating agreement.** The effectiveness of these agreements is hinged on the input and commitment of all members to both create and pledge themselves to following them.

Team leaders and team members who invest time as part of their team norming, will reap the benefits of higher member engagement, efficiency and productivity. As a result, team members will be able to proactively express their communication styles, collaboration preferences, challenges they face and cultural differences that might lead to potential misunderstandings.

Did You Know?
28% of U.S. employees believe their team does NOT build relationships while working together to accomplish tasks.

Teams that have members who are not clear about how the work is done (or who have unenforced norms), invariably get into trouble. Team Operating Agreements are a tool that describe how team members communicate and do their work together. A report by the Institute of Leadership & Management (ILM) "Going Remote: Leading dispersed teams" found that 83% of remote workers struggled with inconsistent working practices and miscommunication, while 83% felt overwhelmed by emails.[7] Taking the time to create a TOA allows virtual team leaders and members to establish clear communication protocols and work goals. I offer teams I support an online

TOA template that allows them to customize it to fit their unique needs. To access the full assessment, visit www.partnersindevelopment.net.

Onboarding

I mentioned earlier that a TOA is ideally created as part of an onboarding process. The Society for Human Resources Management (SHRM) defines onboarding as, "the process of helping new hires adjust to social and performance aspects of their new jobs quickly and smoothly." This is what we want to happen as new virtual teams are formed or as new members join the team.

The first team meeting is critical for laying the foundation for how team members can best work together to achieve results. For newly formed teams, nothing builds trust faster than having a face-to-face meeting. **If your virtual team can have only one face-to-face meeting, make it the first one.**

The first team meeting isn't just about establishing work processes and protocols. It is also about building trust among team members. This is particularly important for global virtual teams who have members from different cultures or who speak different first languages. Different cultures have different values about trust, decision making, hierarchy, feedback and persuasion of groups. A face-to-face meeting is the fastest way to build trust and alignment behind the team's purpose and goals. If a face-to-face meeting is not possible, use video conferencing to allow everyone to see each other.

Did You Know?
35% of U.S. employees are uncomfortable having informal conversations with team members.

Onboarding is a key step to getting your virtual teams started in the right direction. Here are some tips for onboarding virtual team members:

- **Build rapport with team members.** Set aside time for team members to share information about themselves — both work and non-work related. This builds relationships necessary to create high trust.
- **Discuss with members the team's purpose, vision and goals.** Repeat often and ask team members to put these elements into their own words to ensure understanding and alignment.
- **Define member roles and determine how each role interconnects** with other team member roles.

- **Create an onboarding plan** that includes information about the team member's job, the organization, key contacts and technology training.
- **Post team member pictures and/or brief bios or personal videos** where each person introduces themselves to the team. This can be done in the project management site like Slack, team website or on another collaboration site such as Microsoft Sharepoint.
- **Invite stakeholders to share their perspectives** as to why the team is important to the organization and to customers.

PRODUCE

5. Ensure high-quality leader and member communication

Among the many challenges faced by virtual teams, building trusting relationships, managing conflict and creating participation and engagement are at the top of the list.

In a face-to-face conversation, all parties involved exchange meaning through their words, tone of voice and body language (nonverbal signals). Research by Albert Mehrabian suggests that listeners place far more emphasis on tone of voice (as much as 38%) and nonverbals (as much as 55%) particularly when these are incongruent with the spoken words.[8] In the absence of visual observation in a virtual communication exchange, participants have only words and tone of voice from which to derive meaning, and this is where we begin to see an increase in misunderstandings. With text-based communication, emotions are inferred (and often misinterpreted) using words alone. Add multitasking to the mix and it's no wonder why communication, engagement and lack of trust are major obstacles for virtual teams. This is especially true for global virtual teams whose members frequently come from different cultures with different first languages.

Did You Know?

42% of U.S. employees are fearful that their words are being misinterpreted when communicating with their team.

High performance in virtual teams requires all participants to be precise in their communications, to apply strong listening skills, and to make time to build trusting relationships based equally on task-oriented and socially-oriented components. Virtual team leaders need to find ways to engage the hearts and minds of their team members — individually and collectively. Leaders also need to become masters at leading virtual team meetings.

There are two categories of effective virtual team communication — technology and people. Advances in communication and collaboration technology have enabled virtual teams and the mobile workforce to connect to on-site groups and each other anytime and from nearly anywhere in the world. A study by Qualtrics and Accel found that Millennials check their smartphones 150 times per day.[9] Add to that, by 2020, nearly half (46%) of all U.S. Workers will be Millennials.[10]

Yet, with the myriad of technological tools available, none can compensate for people skills associated with virtual presence and emotional intelligence. To communicate effectively, both are needed.

The Technical Side of Communication

Virtual communication and collaboration technologies are becoming more dynamic and less expensive each year. Mobile technologies are also growing and will play an even greater role in connecting virtual team members and storing documents that can be accessed by anyone at any time. The keys to leveraging the right communication technology are twofold: 1) match the method to the message and 2) make sure team members have equal access and know how to use the technology. I will provide some examples on when to use which technology shortly.

> ### *Did You Know?*
> 30% of employees believe their team does
> not have the right technology
> to communicate and be productive.

Communications technology typically falls into two primary types—synchronous (same time) and asynchronous (different time). Both types have their place. Examples of each technology type are shown in the table below:

High Social Presence (Synchronous Technologies)	Low Social Presence (Asynchronous Technologies)
• On-demand collaboration • Online meetings and webconferencing • Videoconferencing • Instant messaging • Telephony • Video calling and conferencing • Desktop sharing • High-definition and telepresence applications	• E-mail • Document sharing and file management • Social networks • Extranets • Enterprise search • Voice and text messaging • Online document collaboration tools • Project management tools

While there are many ways to communicate a message, it is crucial to match the *method* to the *message*. When communicating virtually, two factors should drive your selection of technology — social presence and information richness.

Social presence = personal connection - social presence is the degree to which the communication method creates a personal and emotional connection between the sender and the receiver(s). Methods high in social presence include face-to-face conversations and meetings, video conferences and phone conversations. Email, text messages, and document sharing have a lower social presence. Ambiguous situations, or ones that involve emotions are best resolved using methods high in social presence. Otherwise, low social presence is better because it can reduce the emphasis on interpersonal distractions, such as appearance, accents or other interactions which can interfere with one's objectivity.

Information richness = the amount and variety of information - information richness is the degree to which a communication method helps reinforce the meaning of a message while reducing confusion or misunderstanding. Videoconferencing is high in information richness because it incorporates speech, facial expressions, body language and location. Conversely, a text message or a shared document lacks the richness and context of face-to-face conferencing.

How can you determine which communication technologies are best for your team? Team size and budget may guide your selection for web or cloud-based technologies, collaborative virtual workspaces and data visualization tools. Regardless of your choice, let these two rules guide your decision process:

1) Make sure the technologies you choose are available to all team members. In some countries, cell phones and mobile apps are the primary means of virtual communication. In other countries, the same mobile apps may not be accessible, so before selecting an application for the team, do some checking to ensure equal availability.

2) Make sure all team members know how to use the technology. The biggest reason many technologies don't get used is that team members either don't know how or aren't comfortable using them. This is particularly true of video-based technology. Make time to provide training and practice so that you can fully leverage the power of your technology.

The People Side of Communications

My first leadership experience occurred at age eight. I was in charge of leading a group from one location to another. This group was very different from me, as they had a different language, came from a different culture and had their own way of doing things. While they were familiar with the area we were crossing, they weren't interested in following me. So, instead, I had to learn how to lead from behind by providing guidance, by identifying the team leader, by listening and by noticing their nonverbal communication.

I grew up on a cattle ranch in South Dakota. My first lessons in leadership came not from a group of people, but from a herd of cattle that I was responsible for leading from the pasture to the barn. Those skills of listening, paying attention to nonverbals, looking for the informal leaders in the group and providing guidance have also helped me to lead teams of people, as well. Clearly, there are differences, but when it comes to good communication — virtual or otherwise, the basics still apply. So, let's talk about the key differences between virtual and in-person communication, emotional intelligence and trust.

Emotional intelligence is described as the awareness and the management of our own emotions, noticing the emotional signals of others and using this awareness to create positive, constructive relationships. This is an important skill for the leaders and members of high-performing virtual teams. Building strong and trusting relationships from a distance requires team members and leaders to possess keen listening skills, to acknowledge and express their feelings, and to adapt to different people and situations that may be very different from their own personal histories.

A training icebreaker I often use at the beginning of a face-to-face session is to ask people who don't know each other to stand together back-to-back and interview their partner so that they can later introduce them to the whole group. If you try this icebreaker, you will notice how people respond. Often, some can't resist at least turning sideways to catch a glimpse of their partner as some listen more intently and some make notes. They pay attention to tone of voice and are clearer in how they describe themselves to their partner. It is this intentional listening, sharing and adapting that are key to building relationships between and among virtual team members and leaders.

A study of over 8,000 people employed in businesses. hospitals, universities, the military and government agencies found that the average person listens at only about 25% efficiency.[11] That means that we miss about 75% of what people are telling us and they only hear about 25% of what we're telling them. In a phone conference, where multitasking is rampant, it is no wonder these meetings are not very effective.

A few years ago, I was working with a group of young leaders in Saudi Arabia. We were in class together for eight weeks and one of my students, Abdulrahman, spoke English with a very thick Arabian accent. On the very last day of class, as we were all saying goodbye, Abdulrahman came up to me and said what I thought was, "Thank you, I hope I see you dead!" I looked at him, paused for moment and asked, "Could you repeat that?" When he did, I understood him clearly say, "Thank you. I hope I see you again." I was glad I'd asked him to repeat his words. Never underestimate the importance of listening.

Trust

The greatest struggle for virtual teams is building trusting relationships among their members. Members of face-to-face teams often build in time to get to know one another before delving into the pressures of completing tasks and tight deadlines. Some virtual teams skip past this step, and there is a price to pay for doing so. Lost productivity, unclear expectations, poor quality, conflicts and inability to be heard are cited as areas that are prevalent in teams with low trust.

It is important to note there are two types of trust — cognitive trust and emotional trust. Both are necessary for teams and are developed via unique behaviors.

Cognitive trust is based on logic. That is, it develops based on calculative assessments of one's perceived integrity and ability. You may find yourself wondering, does this team member know what she is doing? Does he have expertise in this area? Can I count on her to deliver what she promised? Can I rely that the information he provided is accurate and based on facts? These are the types of questions we subconsciously ask ourselves to assess whether or not we can trust another. Our trust account with that person grows as we receive positive responses to these questions and it diminishes when we do not. To gain cognitive trust with others, I recommend you follow what I call the Four Cs: credibility, consistency, communication and consideration.

- **Credibility** - demonstrate your expertise to build confidence in your judgment and abilities with your team members
- **Consistency** - do what you say you will do; this allows team members to see you as predictable and reliable

- **Communication** - let team members know what you expect and be flexible and willing to negotiate, if necessary
- **Consideration** - show respect for others needs and follow team-based agreements

---

Did You Know?

14% of employees believe they are a member of a virtual team that does not respect them.

Emotional trust is based on the social bonds between people where there is genuine care and concern for each other. While some individuals are initially more trusting than others, emotional trust typically develops after cognitive trust and via social and informal interactions. When team members both show a professional and personal interest in one another and are willing to share things about themselves beyond task-based conversations, they discover personal commonalities and connections that become the threads of trusting relationships. They are also likely to discover differences, which can add interest and variety to their relationships. This is particularly likely in teams whose members come from a variety of national cultures and backgrounds. To gain emotional trust, one must:

- **Express interest in others**
  "Wow! You really know a lot about marketing. How did you develop this expertise?"

- **Ask questions and really listen**
  "It sounds like you are really busy. What's a typical day like for you? What are some of your challenges? Can I tell you one of mine?"

- **Share non-work interests**
  "I heard you mention on the call the other day that you enjoy cooking. I like to cook, too. What are some of the foods you most like to cook? My family's favorite dish I make is ..."

- **Offer praise, encouragement, and assistance, if needed**
  "This section of the report is just what we need. I know this wasn't easy for you to complete in the short timeline, but you did it. Thank you! I have a little extra time next week, I'd be happy to help with the final section if you'd like."

Trust is the fabric that holds virtual team members together. Without it, goals are more difficult to accomplish, and results are ultimately compromised. Team leaders and team members need to invest time and attention to build trust within their teams. To do this in a virtual environment, consider these additional suggestions in the following table:

Team Leader to Team Member Trust	Team Member to Team Member Trust
• Communicate openly and honestly to model transparency • Hold regular one-on-one coaching and feedback conversations with each team member • Jointly create team member development plans and meet face-to-face at least annually • Positively reinforce effective team member behaviors and results - privately or publicly based on their personal preferences • Show appropriate personal interest in each team member • Learn about the culture and customs of global team members • Share personal interests outside of work • Ask each team member about their personal reward and recognition preferences • Provide information about the organization and its priorities	• Offer praise and encouragement to each other • Show appropriate personal interest in other team members • Share personal interests outside of work and invite others to share theirs; look for commonalities • Offer assistance and share information that could aid others • Listen, paying attention to words used, subtle cues, tone of voice, and silence • Ask open-ended questions to get team members to expand and explain their answers • Ask close-ended questions to get team members to focus and provide direct responses • Learn about the culture and customs of global team members • Take a short video of you in your office space and share it with team members

Have you ever heard the saying "trust is like money — hard to earn and easy to lose?" Indeed, we make emotional deposits and withdrawals in our trust accounts with others every day. We must be cautious not to overdraw those accounts and lose all trust from our team members.

Cognitive trust can be earned and lost (like money). As you accumulate a balance, you gain emotional trust (like gaining interest on your money) that supports you when you make withdrawals. For example, you must have high trust to make the following request of a team member: "Bob, I need to have a special report completed ASAP. I'm sorry I can't give you the details now. Please trust that I have a valid reason for asking."

In the case of James and Su Min, a valuable team member was lost because of a lack of trust and misunderstanding of team member values and preferences.

6. Maintain high productivity and engagement

According to Gallup Daily tracking, 32% of employees in the U.S. are engaged - meaning they are involved in, enthusiastic about and committed to their work and workplace. Worldwide, only 13% of employees working for an organization are engaged."[12] In a 2017 Gallup study, it is estimated that "disengaged employees cost the country somewhere between $450 and $550 billion each year."[13]

Engagement has a high correlation to productivity. The higher the engagement, the higher the productivity. Unfortunately, the reverse is also true. Engagement is defined as the emotional and functional commitment one has to his or her organization. High engagement requires high trust and team leaders hold the keys to developing, managing and guarding this trust on their teams. As the old saying goes, "people don't leave organizations, they leave their managers."

With a majority of U.S. employees today working remotely at least part-time, leaders must both understand and apply the skills that foster team member engagement in a virtual environment. What are those skills? Let's first look at what virtual team members want from their leaders. Here is some feedback I've received from virtual team members I have trained:

- **Keith:** "I want to understand the connections; connections between my work, the team's work and our organization. What are we ultimately contributing to?"
- **Norah:** "Team meetings are often a waste of time. They're not well planned, people aren't prepared, and the same people always speak up. What's the point? I'm so

busy, I try to do other work when the topics don't concern me."

- **Satchiko:** "We try to use the technology to be more efficient and engaged, but some team members don't know how to use it. Many don't want to turn on their webcams because they don't want others to see if their hair is messy or whatever. It's not engaging to stare at a blank screen."

- **Javier:** "I want to grow and develop my skills, advance myself. How can I do that when I work remotely and seldom connect directly with others in the company?"

- **Fernando:** "Team meetings are always held at the same time which is during office hours for some people. For me, it's 2:00 in the morning and for others, it's 7:00 in the evening. Why are we the ones who always have to meet outside of regular working hours?"

- **Dominique:** "I'd like to have input in the decisions that directly affect me and my work. I understand that leaders must make some decisions, but I'd at least like to be asked for my opinion."

- **Rana:** "I'd like to get to know my team members better. We're always so busy, we never seem to have time to get to know each other. I think this would help us work better together."

From these comments, you are likely to gain an understanding of some of the areas that cause disengagement among team members.

Here are ten ways you can continue to engage virtual team members and boost productivity:

Creating Engagement

1. Connect the team's purpose, vision, and goals to those of the larger organization. Help team members see the unique value they contribute and why their work is important.

2. Provide clear direction, yet be flexible. Author Stephen Covey said, "Begin with the end in mind." When applying this sentiment to virtual leadership, virtual team leaders must remember to be very explicit in their communication, especially when it comes to setting goals and direction. With global virtual teams, misunderstandings can easily arise due to language and cultural differences. For example, in some cultures, the word "yes" means "I heard what you said", and not, "I agree with you."

I find that leaders (both onsite and virtual) often hesitate to provide the clear direction their team members need to develop new skills. Yet, especially when learning new skills, team members need information about what to do, how to do it, when, with whom and where. Without clear direction, team members will flounder, become frustrated, resentful and disengaged. Because each team member is different, leaders will need to be flexible in their communication style and approach. By not providing clear direction, which takes extra effort when leading virtually, leaders are missing opportunities to build the skills and engage their team members.

3. Connect engagement to high performance. Engagement is directly tied to performance. If we want our team members to be involved in, enthusiastic about and committed to their work and workplace, virtual leaders model the way. Start by asking yourself these questions:

- *On a scale of 1 to 5 (1 = low and 5 = high), how engaged are you in your team's work?*
- *What's your tone of voice during team meetings?*
- *On a scale of 1 to 5 (1 = low and 5 = high), how enthusiastic are you about the work your virtual team members complete?*
- *Do you positively reinforce and recognize team members (in they way they prefer) for good performance?*

Leaders who are engaged and enthusiastic when communicating with their virtual teams will see noticeably higher performance results in their remote workers than those who do not.

4. Create clear working agreements such as a Team Operating Agreement that describes how the team will communicate, make decisions, resolve conflicts, etc. Acknowledge any cultural differences and find agreements that work for everyone. Review the agreement periodically to check progress.

Did You Know?
34% of employees do not believe their virtual team can come to a consensus without conflict.

---

5. Make time to build relationships with each individual member and foster these among team members. Include a few minutes at the beginning of team meetings and during one-on-one conversations to discuss topics not directly related to work tasks to show personal interest. For example, questions like, "Tell me about something fun you've done recently? What's something good that's happened this week? What are you looking forward to this weekend?" suggest a personal interest in others. They prompt conversations that lead to a better understanding of each other and engage people's hearts as well as their minds.

6. Track and assess progress, then celebrate milestones and successes. Out of sight, out of mind is a frequent concern expressed by remote workers and their leaders. Leaders sometimes wonder to what extent their team members are 'really working' when they can't directly observe them. Team members worry that their accomplishments are often overlooked or discounted compared to their co-workers located onsite. That's why it's important to identify individual and team milestones of progress. I describe these as lead and lag indicators of performance.

Lead indicators are typically team member behaviors used to obtain results. They include the extent to which team members take accountability for their actions, listen attentively and offer constructive feedback. When demonstrated, these skills lead to positive results. **Lag indicators** are the outputs or results of individual and collective team member behaviors. They include quantitative measures such as productivity goals, quality and service standards, and accomplishments. To maintain high engagement and performance, tracking milestones along the way and celebrating successes is key. We will discuss more on lead and lag indicators in Chapter 3.

7. Hold people accountable for the right behaviors and directly address destructive behaviors. Team member behaviors are the lead indicators of team relations and engagement. When behaviors such as poor listening, personal attacks or withholding information from others occur, they should be addressed quickly and not allowed to fester. Depending on the circumstances, some of these issues may be addressed during team meetings. For example, if an individual is always the first to respond in team meetings and rarely lets other members get a word in, you might say, "I know you have lots of ideas. Let's hear from some other team members first, then please add your comments after we hear what they have to say." Creating a Team Operating Agreement that defines appropriate behaviors can often prevent such behavior and serve as a reference point for further discussion. Recognize also that there are communication differences among cultures and 'seek first to understand, then be understood.'

8. Conduct regular one-on-one coaching sessions with each team member and include discussions about development interests and opportunities. This is one of the most important engagement and management practices for remote employees, virtual and onsite team members. Coaching sessions are should be structured to be helpful, constructive and developmental. Both team members and leaders are jointly accountable to make these conversations productive. Topics may include brief status updates, problem solving, clarifying goals or relationship-oriented. When team members know they can count on focused time with their leader, they're able to save questions until that time and avoid interruptions that can wait. The bonus for leaders is that one-on-ones actually SAVE time due to fewer interruptions.

9. Involve team members in decisions that directly affect them whenever possible. Team members want to feel that they have some control and input in decisions that impact what results they are to achieve and how to achieve them. They also want to be involved in setting goals, timelines and the means by which their progress and success will be measured. Bypassing this involvement in the interest of time and efficiency usually backfires. Leaders who invest time by including team members in discussions about goals, protocols for decision making and levels of authority save time spent later due to mistakes, misunderstandings and poor relationships.

10. Plan and manage effective team meetings. Leaders who practice these skills and methods will reap the benefits of team members who are, indeed, emotionally and functionally committed to their work, their team and their organization. That's engagement!

Virtual Team Meetings

This is such an important aspect of engagement that it deserves a place of its own.

Over the past ten years, virtual meetings have become the new normal. There are more meetings conducted virtually than are held with all members physically in the same location. Yet, we also know that engagement levels in virtual meetings drop considerably — especially in meetings that are audio only. In hybrid meetings (where some members are co-located and others connect virtually), engagement drops even more as the lure of multi-tasking becomes just too much to resist.

Effective Virtual Team Meetings

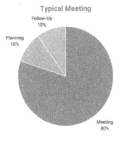

Typical Meeting

Follow-Up 10%

Planning 10%

Meeting 80%

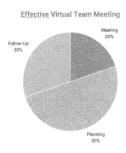

Effective Virtual Team Meeting

Meeting 20%

Follow-Up 30%

Planning 50%

In my consulting experiences, business teams have noted that as little as 10% of the time spent in a typical face-to-face meeting is devoted to planning and later following up afterwards. A best practice is to spend more time advance planning for virtual meetings. This includes creating agendas that state the expected outcomes of the meeting, preparing the technology to be used (such as polls, group chats, etc.), and providing information in advance so that team members are prepared to discuss topics and make decisions. After the meeting, team leaders should follow up to ensure there is clear understanding and commitment to responsibilities. This reduces the time people spend in meetings and increases engagement.

Virtual Team Meeting Checklist: Here is my checklist you may find helpful for increasing engagement. Tally the number of your "Yes" and "No" responses to check the quality of your meetings. You can also find this checklist in my online resource center at **LiterallyVirtually.com.**

Before the Meeting	Yes	No
1. Did you draft the meeting agenda? Include the meeting purpose, topics, expected outcomes (decision, action, FYI), who needs to attend, and estimated time for each topic. Include 5-10 minutes at the beginning of each meeting for socializing to build rapport.		

Before the Meeting	Yes	No
2. Did you determine the technology methods that best match the messages to be communicated? Confirm that participants have the required technology and bandwidth needed.		
3. Did you ensure that all participants know how to use the required technology?		
4. Did you determine the meeting length and time of day? Limit meetings to 60-90 minutes; if longer, plan a break. Rotate meeting times when multiple time zones are involved.		
5. Did you send out the agenda and meeting materials in advance? Expect participants to have read the materials prior to the meeting and are prepared to engage.		
6. Did you leverage technology engagement tools — group chat, polls, screen sharing, etc?		
7. Did you upload presentation materials in advance and test the technology? Have a backup plan?		
8. Did you delegate tasks such as taking meeting minutes, presenting a topic and soliciting input?		

During the Meeting	Yes	No
9. Did you begin with a question to engage everyone? Have members say their names when speaking.		
10. Did you recap the meeting purpose, time, and expectations?		
11. Did you ask participants to close their laptops and place their mobile devices on silent while the meeting is in progress?		
12. Did you vary your voice pace, tone and pitch to engage participants and gain involvement?		
13. Did you use a "parking lot" for any items that are important but outside of the agenda?		
14. Did you ask one question at a time and wait 10 seconds for members to respond?		
15. Did you listen for voice tone and word choice to understand the meaning behind words?		
16. Did you prevent individuals from dominating the meeting? Solicit input from members who are quiet. Use a "round robin" technique to solicit input. Do not assume that silence means agreement. Allow for anonymous feedback.		

	Yes	No
17. Did you record meetings for those unable to attend?		
After the Meeting	**Yes**	**No**
18. Did you post meeting notes and the recording (if used) and notify participants?		
19. Did you post any action items, due dates, and responsibilities on the team website?		
20. Did you solicit member feedback about meetings and what would make them better?		
21. Did you call or email participants to ensure understanding, follow-through and commitment to the meeting outcomes?		
22. Did you brief absent members after they view meeting notes or listen to the recording?		
23. Did you prepare participants for the next meeting?		
TOTALS		

How did you do? The more "yes" answers you have, the more likely that your team members will find virtual meetings more engaging and more productive. Virtual team meetings don't have to be more time consuming, but they do have to be different. Investing time before and after enables you to focus on what's really important to gain from the meeting and save time in the long run.

The Produce phase (when achieved) results in team synergy that can be expressed with this equation:

(High Communication) x
(Personal Engagement) = **Team Synergy**

Because synergy is the product of these elements, anything less than 100% in either high communication or personal engagement yields low virtual team synergy. Both are required for high performance. As leaders of virtual teams and mobile workers, we need to practice the skills and methods that lead team members to engage and optimize their contributions.

RESULTS

7. Provide performance support

Performance support is about having the people, processes and technology in place to provide timely feedback to virtual team leaders and members. Moreover, performance support also aids stakeholders outside of the team whose support (or lack of it) can significantly influence its overall success.

Stakeholder Support

Businessdictionary.com defines a "stakeholder" as "a person, group or organization that has interest or concern in an organization." Stakeholders may be anyone inside or outside of the organization who could be affected by group actions, objectives and policies. For virtual teams, stakeholders may include senior executives, direct supervisors of team members, leaders of other business divisions/department, unions and outside suppliers.

Too often, stakeholders' communication needs and support are not fully considered, and that can lead to problems! Have you identified the stakeholders for your team? Are you confident of their support? Keep in mind, that support includes acting on the team's behalf to cross organizational barriers, provide resources, serve as a link to upper management and resolve conflicts of interest.

For temporary teams, performance support from stakeholders ideally begins before the team is formed. This begins with identifying the various stakeholder individuals and groups whose support is critical to the team's success. Once stakeholders are identified, I strongly recommend creating a **Stakeholders Communication Agreement**.

A Stakeholders Communication Agreement enables the team to proactively manage its communications with sponsors, champions and other stakeholders who support the team. It also serves to manage expectations and provide essential information about the team's progress as milestones are achieved and to communicate issues and obstacles that may require additional input or support.

A stakeholder communications agreement includes:

- Stakeholders by name, their role, and relationship to the team (e.g. Sponsor, Champion, Stakeholder groups or other stakeholders whose support and assistance is important to the team)
- Information needs of each stakeholder, which are the types of information they require to support the team
- Communication methods and frequency by which each stakeholder wishes to receive information e.g. emails, progress reports, video conferences, etc.

A sample of a Stakeholders Communication Agreement is provided in my online resource center at **LiterallyVirtually.com.**

Did You Know?
Only 65% of employees who work in virtual teams believe they are able to correctly interpret team member emails, texts and IMs.

A periodic review of stakeholders and their communication needs is helpful to maintain communications and support. Stakeholders and circumstances frequently change. Maintaining regular communication to inform stakeholders of the team's progress is a proactive approach to strong team support. If yours is a temporary team, share with stakeholders the final results of the team's work and invite them to join in celebrating success.

Track and Assess Team Progress

One of the things that keeps virtual team leaders awake at night is tracking and assessing team member performance. Virtual leaders often ask themselves, "If I can't see my team members, how do I know if they are really working?" Virtual team members may also wonder, "Does my leader really understand and appreciate what I do or is it 'out of sight, out of mind'?" If both of these questions are likely in a team, performance may suffer and team member engagement is likely to plummet. This is especially true for team members who work remotely 100% of the time.

Did You Know?
57% of employees have no clear
measures in place to assess individual
and team performance.

According to studies done by Gallup, team members who work remotely average four more work hours per week than their onsite counterparts.[14] Yet, our research indicates that more than half (57%) of virtual employees have no clear measures in place to assess individual and team performance. And 45% say their team has no tool or system to track milestones. How do you assess and track the performance of your remote team members? I suspect that Shonda had not considered this.

When it comes to tracking and assessing performance, there are two types of indicators — **lead indicators** and **lag indicators.**

Lag indicators are the "after-the-event" outputs that can serve as the quantitative and qualitative signposts of results achieved. Examples of these include balanced scorecard postings, stakeholder feedback, project management Gantt charts and production reports.

Lead indicators are team member behaviors and work processes that provide predictive information about how team members are interacting and completing work activities/tasks that lead to measurable results. These include number of sales calls made, observation, one-on-one coaching conversations, participation in team meetings, and team trust audits.

By differentiating and tracking lead and lag indicators, leaders and team members can both be proactive in monitoring progress (or detecting issues before they become serious problems). The indicators become a feedback mechanism that enables teams to identify and make small course corrections before they become major ones. Perhaps if Shonda and her team had determined their lead and lag indicators early, they might not be faced with their current situation.

Coach and Incentivize

As we are faced with busier workdays, it is easy to assume that if a team member needs something from us, they will get in touch. In virtual teams, where there are significant differences in time, distance, technology and culture, this is a faulty assumption.

In our research, only 47% of employees reported that they received regular feedback and coaching they needed to stay productive and engaged with their team. The absence of regular feedback and coaching too often leads to missed deadlines, lack of productivity, and lower morale." I am a strong advocate of holding regular one-on-one coaching conversations with team members. In a virtual environment, these conversations serve as a lifeline between leaders and team members and provide an opportunity to build trusting relationships, as well as needed guidance to achieving goals.

Did You Know?

32% of employees said they did NOT establish trust with their team during the first meeting.

These one-on-one coaching conversations are intended to be constructive, developmental and helpful. They should occur regularly — at least monthly, weekly or biweekly — and early as the team is formed and again as new members are brought on board. These meetings can be relatively short – 30 minutes to an hour. Leaders who remain vigilant in scheduling time for the one-on-ones, find that not only do they yield team members who are more proactive and engaged, but these leaders save time as they experience fewer interruptions with team members who can solve more problems on their own.

Finally, performance incentives should be personalized based on individual team member preferences. While some team members enjoy public recognition, that is not true for everyone, as James learned with Su Min. Awareness of cultural differences as well as individual preferences can avoid such consequences.

Generational differences also matter to how team members wish to be recognized. According to Human Resource Executive Online, Generation Y workers are much less likely than Baby Boomers to believe that working harder and taking more responsibility will get recognized and rewarded by the organization.[15] The most important thing to remember about recognizing and incentivizing top performance is to personalize it – make it genuine and meaningful to the individual.

8. Deliver timely results

The uncontested measure of a virtual team's effectiveness is their ability to deliver high quality, timely results. Over the years, there has been a steady increase in the performance levels of virtual teams. A 2009 study of 80 global software teams by authors from the Boston Consulting Group and WHU - Otto Beisheim School of Management found that well-managed dispersed teams can actually outperform those that share office space.[16] Similarly, an Aon Consulting report noted that using virtual teams can improve employee productivity; some organizations have seen gains of up to 43%.[16]

Did You Know?
15% of employees state that their team does not deliver high quality results on time.

Despite this data, many virtual teams do not achieve these levels, in part, due to a lack of recognition and celebrating the milestones that lead to successful results. In our research, 46% of virtual team members said they are not recognized individually for their contributions (according to their preferences) and 40% said their team does not celebrate milestones or accomplishments. When combined with a lack of clear performance measures and a means to track milestones, we can see why team members become disengaged and some teams fail to achieve high performance.

Recognizing and rewarding virtual team member behaviors and results requires a genuine desire to acknowledge positive contributions to the team and providing specific feedback so that members are clear about what they did that led to the recognition. Often, leaders are too general in their feedback and team members are left wondering exactly what they're being recognized for.

Instead of: *Aisha, good job on the analytics.*

Try: *Hamad, your prototype of the customer service software really brings to life how we can better serve our customers.*

Positive feedback goes a long way to raising engagement by reinforcing the behaviors (lead indicators) that contribute to results (lag indicators).

> ### *Did You Know?*
> *Only 47% of employees receive regular feedback and coaching needed to stay productive and engaged with their team.*

It is important for virtual team leaders to differentiate between recognition and rewards in their groups. Rewards are commonly associated with some financial component such as a spot bonus, paid time off or a small gift that has meaning to the receiver. Conversely, recognition may have little or no financial component, but offers a sincere and meaningful acknowledgement of a team member's contributions. Recognizing and rewarding virtual team members sometimes requires a little extra of creativity and should be culturally appropriate. Again, they are most meaningful when they are based on individual team member preferences. If you are in doubt about what your team would prefer, ask members how they prefer to be recognized. This could even be a topic of discussion for a team meeting. Had James done that, Su Min could have shared with him her preferences and avoided what she felt was a humiliating rather than a rewarding experience.

To get you started in your thinking, this table offers some ideas for ways to recognize and reward virtual team members:

Recognition	Rewards
• Handwritten 'thank you' notes • Letter of recognition placed in personnel file • Verbal thank you (in private or in front of others, depending on their preference) • Acknowledge and celebrate birthdays; have a piece of birthday cake delivered to virtual team members' locations • Plan a surprise "milestone achievement" celebration as a part of a virtual team meeting • Send a note of thanks to the team member's home address and their direct supervisor • Send an award plaque or certificate of appreciation • Ask team members to contribute photos and create a photo collage of a successful project that shows the people who worked on it • Phone call a team member to thank them	• Hold a virtual lunch (or other meal) with your team member; arrange to have lunch delivered to their office and connect via a web conference • Express interest in the team member's career goals • Paid time off • Gift certificates/cards • Movie, theater, or sports tickets • Spot bonus • Small gift that has meaning to the receiver • Award plaque or certificate of appreciation • Provide a business-related gift • (e.g. pen, business card holder, portfolio, etc.) • Items with company logo (mugs, t-shirts, caps, etc.) • Contribution to team member's favorite charity • Arrange for team members to attend professional development conferences or courses

There are many books and online resources for additional ideas to recognize and reward high performance behaviors and results (see my online resource center at **LiterallyVirtually.com.**).[17]

High-performing teams not only complete milestones, they recognize positive team member behaviors, they deliver timely results, and they celebrate successes. And in the process, most team members report having fun! Do not miss these opportunities to breathe life into your team.

Eight Predictors of High Performance

In summary, here are the key drivers of high virtual team performance. Your ability to execute on these differentiators is the difference between having an average-performing virtual team and a high-performing virtual team. How many of these are present in your current team?

In the next chapter, we will look deeper into Shonda's team to determine what could have been done differently to build this team in order to deliver a compelling business expansion proposal to upper management of EMCA Foodservice, Inc. In the process, you will discover some things that will help your teams, too.

CHAPTER 3

Examining and Establishing Team Culture

Shonda and her team have found themselves in a bit of a mess. They are just a few short days away from their first major presentation of a business development plan to senior leaders for the global expansion of EMCA Foodservice's foodservice company. As Shonda watched the chaos and conflict among team members during their first face-to-face meeting, she found herself momentarily tuning out the disruption and wondering how things could have been done differently to create the outcome she'd hoped for — one that was very different from what she was observing.

Initially, Shonda believed her team members were clear about the team's purpose and vision, including goals and priorities. She felt that the members she selected had the right skills and could quickly develop trusting relationships to enable them to communicate openly and collaboratively. She also hoped that when disagreements occurred, her team could apply emotional intelligence skills to listen and understand one another to find the best solutions to tackle any problems. Finally, she imagined that her team could create and follow protocols for working together and the end result would be that they hit their milestones and achieve performance results on time or ahead of the deadline. Now, as Shonda watched the scene before her eyes, she wondered what went wrong that brought them to this point in time.

As a leader and members of a global virtual team, Shonda's team is not alone in their challenges. In a 2016 survey report by RW3 CultureWizard, only 22% of 1,372 respondents (from 80 countries), participated in virtual team training, and only 34% in formal global leadership training.[18] Additional survey results revealed:

- Of the respondents who identified themselves as **global team leaders**, 96% rated themselves as either effective or highly effective at leading multicultural teams; however, 58% of respondents (who were participants on teams) rated their global team leaders as **not adequately prepared** to lead multicultural teams.

- 68% reported that **cultural challenges** were the biggest hurdle to global team productivity.
- Only 28% had a **team charter** (Team Operating Agreement) or used guidelines to achieve high performance.
- 41% of the teams **never meet in person**, 28% meet once a year and 31% meet twice a year.
- 36% of respondents identified themselves as leaders of global virtual teams; of those, only 2-4% **felt uncomfortable leading global virtual teams**.

The Impacts of Physical Distance, Time, Technology and Culture on a Virtual Workforce

It would be wishful thinking to believe that the challenges faced by Shonda and her team are unusual or uncommon. Today, more people telecommute, work remotely, or are leaders and members of virtual teams—many of which are global virtual teams—than ever before. And the skills required are different from those of teams whose members are located onsite and near one another. The challenges of dealing with differences in geography, culture, technology and multiple time zones are enough to rattle even the most senior leaders.

Let's start by describing the different types of workers and team members who make up this virtual workforce.

"I Can Work Anywhere"

In general, these individuals work remotely. They may work from home, travel a great deal ("my office is my car"), or work alone at another location--even if in a similar vicinity. They communicate largely via electronic means, and seldom, if ever, meet face-to- face. They may be 100% remote or may work part-time at an office and the remainder of time off-site. Typically, their work tasks are relatively independent of others. Examples include virtual office assistants, contractors or vendors who offer specific services, and employees who provide data entry or services to a select group of customers. While these individuals may connect with others (including their leader) occasionally to share information, receive direction and provide feedback, they do not frequently interact with others outside the scope of their work.

"We Work Together, but in Other Places" (Virtual Teams)

These individuals are, indeed, members of a team whose work and collective performance require collaboration, communication, and shared goals.

Team members are not co-located and also communicate largely via electronic means, and seldom, if ever meet face-to-face. They may be 100% remote or may work part-time off-site and only occasionally at an office with their co-workers. While some teams' members are geographically closer, global virtual team members are separated by large geographic differences, across multiple time zones (6 or more hours apart), culture, and access to technology.

"Some of Us Work Together and Some of Us Work Apart" (Hybrid Teams)

Hybrid teams include members who are co-located (onsite) as well as virtual members. These teams face challenges, too. It's not uncommon for the virtual team members to feel that members onsite have advantages of closer access to their leaders, more frequent face-to-face interactions, and greater access to organizational information and social activities. Onsite team members sometimes view their virtual colleagues as having the advantages of more flexibility in their work schedules, fewer interruptions, and the ability to work in whatever clothes they decide to put on that day.

The truth is there are advantages and disadvantages to all aspects and types of the virtual workforce. Leaders of remote workers and virtual (and hybrid) teams find it to be more time consuming and complex to create high performing teams that meet or surpass the performance of onsite teams.

Research conducted by RW3 Culture Wizard indicates that managing conflict, making decisions and expressing opinions are extremely more challenging for virtual teams.[19] With these challenges, it is not surprising that virtual teams find it more difficult to make decisions. And that's only part of the story.

Some of the top challenges of virtual teams include:

- Building trust from a distance
- Leveraging communications technology
- Underestimating cultural differences
- Aligning members behind the team's purpose and vision
- Creating and maintaining engagement
- Balancing structure and empowerment
- Tracking and assessing performance
- Making the implicit, explicit

But there is also good news! Many organizations find that, when well-managed, virtual teams can deliver high quality, innovative products and services that meet or exceed expectations. And, this trend is expected to continue as more and more members gain experience operating in a virtual work environment. In a research study conducted by the Business Research Consortium virtual teams have become an essential way of getting work done well. The study found that virtual teams are best at improving quality and meeting (or exceeding) goals.[20]

To be specific, they found that virtual teams can:

- Improve the quality of work
- Meet or exceed goals
- Increase worker productivity
- Innovate products and services
- Support corporate culture
- Raise employee engagement levels

Those who work remotely 60-80% of the time but spend some time in the office are among the highest engaged employees. That's higher than employees who work remotely 100% of the time (least engaged) and those who work 100% of the time in an office.[21]

Impacts of Time, Distance, Culture and Technology (and how to avoid stereotypes)

What if Shonda and her team had been able to meet face-to-face? Would the situation they find themselves in be any different? As a global virtual team, these members face some of the greatest challenges in their work together. They are separated by large geographic distances, time zones more than six hours apart, very different first languages and cultures, and varying access to communication and collaboration technologies. While any one of them would require some adaptation by leaders and their team members, combined, they raise exponentially the level of complexity for completing their assignments. When individuals don't have opportunities to get to know one another, personally, they often resort to stereotypes. That can lead to biases and misunderstandings. If not addressed and resolved, conflicts will occur and performance is compromised.

Distance

It has been shown that when the physical distance between two people is 50 feet or more, they modify the way they communicate. Instead of having a face-to-face conversation, they start to rely more on technology. They converse by phone, email or text rather than meet. The resulting impact is they lose access to context (which can also lead to misinterpretations and misunderstandings).

In face-to-face conversations, the individuals have access to not only the words and tone of voice of the other party, they also have the benefit of seeing each other's nonverbal responses. Body language is a major contributor to understanding the true message that's being communicated. For example, say aloud the sentence, "I'm so happy to see you." As you say it each time, change your tone of voice and your body language. You'll find that you are sending a very different message even though the words are the same. Combined, body language and tone of voice can account for a majority of your message. That's why text and email messages so often get interpreted different from what the receiver may have intended. In the absence of context, people naturally add their own—correctly or incorrectly.

Time

Shonda and some of her team members are separated by time differences of roughly 13 hours. Having a team meeting in which everyone can participate means that some members are either staying late or getting up very early. Think of the impact that has on their level of engagement. This becomes even more troublesome when meetings are held at the same time and at the convenience of only some members. Those having to participate outside of regular working hours can become resentful and non-participatory. When that happens, the whole team suffers. That is why rotating meeting times is important. All members get the experience of being equally accommodated and inconvenienced and that builds camaraderie.

Technology

Advances in technology have made communicating and collaborating with virtual team members easier and more efficient than ever. Document sharing, social media, screen sharing and video-conferencing are just of the few tools now at the disposal of virtual team members. The addition of video technology has greatly enhanced virtual teams' abilities to communicate more effectively and strengthen team member relationships. Yet, challenges remain.

One of these challenges is ensuring that everyone has access to the technology. For global virtual teams, there are still technology access issues in some countries. Cell phones are the primary technology mode in some nations, as there is limited access to personal computers. And, high internet fees can make accessibility difficult.

Secondly, the technology that is available is not always fully utilized. The biggest reason is that team members are uncomfortable because they do not know how to use it properly. It has been shown that the use of video, group chats, polls and other engagement tools lead to greater levels of virtual meeting participation and less multi-tasking. Making time to ensure that team members are adept and comfortable using these technologies can greatly enhance productivity and member involvement. Though some team members may be uncomfortable using their webcams to provide a visual connection ("I apologize, I'm having a bad hair day!"), the engagement among members outweighs an individual's reaction to a bad hair day.

Culture

One of the greatest challenges to virtual teams is creating a team culture. That is, a team community that blends the diverse backgrounds of all its members into one that leverages individual strengths and develops shared meanings, effective and efficient communication practices, and respects individual differences. These differences may include age, gender, education and expertise, first language, sexual orientation, hierarchy, religion, national culture and more. Even teams whose members all reside in the same country can experience these differences. And, remember, everyone is an individual who cannot be adequately described by any one group.

Shonda and her team have certainly experienced these challenges. It is not uncommon for team members to lack experience working on virtual teams or have not received training on how to work virtually. This inhibits their ability to fully participate and contribute to their team's mission and goals. In the absence of face-to-face communication, problems associated with these challenges can lie under the surface only to erupt in conflicts that derail team progress and performance. Being an effective virtual team leader and member requires additional skills from those who work onsite. These skills include understanding cultural differences, our own biases, and our ability to create a team culture so that members are focused on how they contribute to high individual and team performance. In the following sections we will discuss ways to create an open dialogue about cultural differences and build a team culture where members freely communicate and engage.

Global Virtual Teams

Monocultural	Multicultural
Stable Membership	Flexible Membership
Single Time Zone	Multiple Time Zones
Common Language	Multiple Languages
Single Function	Multiple Functions

How have these affected you?

Understanding the Complexity and Reliance of Virtual Teams

The differences of distance, time, technology, and culture add to the complexity of leading and being a member of virtual teams. When it comes to working with virtual teams, particularly globally dispersed teams, there are two great truths.

1. The greater the spans of time, distance, technology and culture, the more complex it is for team members to work effectively together.
2. The more that team members must rely on one another to achieve results, the greater the need for trust and alignment behind team purpose.

Complexity

When we refer to the complexity of virtual teams, we are acknowledging the differences among team members related to time zones, geographical distance, access to communications and collaboration technology and national cultures.

How complex is your team? Find out by answering the questions below. If you answer "yes" to a majority of these questions, you are a member of a team with high complexity.

1. Do your team members reside in more than two countries?
2. Do you communicate with members across time zones that are more than six hours apart?
3. Are there more than two national cultures represented by your team?
4. Are there more than two native languages represented by your team?
5. Are there more than two functional areas of your organization represented by your team?
6. Are there differences in access to communication and collaboration technology based on team member location?

A high level of complexity challenges leaders to find different ways to build trust, communicate and achieve results. The old "command and control" leadership approach does not work in these situations.

Reliance

The second great truth is that virtual team members must develop the ability to create trusting relationships with one another, usually without the benefit of meeting face-to-face. It takes more time and effort to develop high levels of trust from a distance. And trust is critical when team members must rely on one another to complete their portions of a work product so that the overall team accomplishes its intended goals.

Reliance describes to the level of interdependence among team members. Some teams have members who are located in the same or different countries, but each team member works relatively independently. For example, a group of pharmaceutical sales representatives who work out of their homes but report to the same regional manager. While they may occasionally have virtual team meetings and share information, their sales results are not dependent on the sales of other representatives. Another example could be a not-for-profit organization that works around the world with each location forming its own goals and teams; or a training team whose members work together but teach different programs in different parts of the world. These are examples considered to be lower in reliance than teams whose work requires higher levels of interdependence among members for input and completing tasks such as Shonda's team.

How much reliance is reflected in your team? Find out by answering the questions below. If you answer "yes" to a majority of these questions, you are part of a team with high reliance.

1. Do your team members need to frequently communicate as a full group to make decisions?
2. Must your team members rely upon the expertise of other members to complete tasks?
3. Does your team need access to all documents and information at all times?
4. Must your team members collaborate to successfully complete projects?
5. Are leadership responsibilities shared among team members (versus a single leader)?
6. Is compensation based on team and individual performance?

If we map complexity and reliance onto a matrix, it looks something like this, with teams that are high in complexity being at the top half of the matrix.

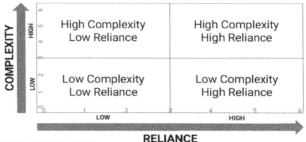

Virtual Team Types
Complexity vs. Reliance

HIGH	High Complexity Low Reliance			High Complexity High Reliance		
LOW	Low Complexity Low Reliance			Low Complexity High Reliance		

COMPLEXITY

LOW — RELIANCE — HIGH

In this matrix, the Complexity axis represents the impact of factors related to time, distance, culture and technology on a team. The Reliance axis represents the level of interdependence among team members.

A **High Complexity/Low Reliance** team is one whose members are separated by large differences in time, distance, culture and technology and the members work relatively independently. While members may connect via technology occasionally to receive updates about the organization and share best practices, their work goals and performance are not as reliant on that of other members. An example of this team type is a group of global marketing directors who report to the same vice president of international marketing and where the directors' marketing initiatives and performance in their country is not dependent on those in other countries. Each marketing director functions independently of the others. Individuals working for an international academic institution with satellite offices globally is another example where the work of members in one country functions separately from others.

For these teams, the leader-to-individual team member relationship is primary. This means building trust, communicating, making decisions and concentrating on individual job performance are the focus. A leader of a team that is high in complexity and low in reliance learns that he/she must come to some agreements with each individual team member as to how they will work together from a distance—leveraging technology, adapting to each other's cultural differences, and agreeing how productivity will be tracked and measured. These will be different for each team member.

High Complexity/High Reliance teams share the same complexity challenges of large differences in time, distance, culture and technology and the associated responsibilities of aligning all team members behind a shared mission, vision and goals. Leaders of these teams must be concerned not only with their relationship with each individual team member, but also focus on building relationships and communication among all team members. This is because their work is highly interdependent on one another. Also, leaders must address how each team member builds trust with other team members, how team decisions are made, how team members share critical information with each other, and how collective productivity is measured. That the overall team performance is the total of both the members' and the leader's individual contributions. That means, a problem for one is a problem for all! High Complexity/High Reliance teams are the most challenging to be a member of and to lead.

While **Low Complexity/High Reliance teams** don't share all the challenges of high complexity teams, they are likely dealing with smaller differences such as fewer time zones, shorter distances, and various members' access and discomfort with technology. Yet, there can be high levels of interdependence within the team, including compensation based on a combination of individual and team performance. A national team that utilizes contract workers who have a specialized expertise needed to complete a project is one example. A hybrid team of IT members, both onsite and remote, who are creating and implementing a new software program for an organization is another. Leaders of these teams share some of the same challenges of other high reliance teams despite the smaller differences in complexity.

Low Complexity/Low Reliance teams may include independent remote and mobile workers, employees who are co-located, and even others who work in the same or different buildings in the same city. While complexity is smaller, even small differences can impact team members' opportunities for face-to-face interactions, access to their leader, and varied engagement levels. Because they work relatively independently, performance is primarily a result of their individual accomplishments. One example of this team type is a group of Human Resource (HR) Generalists, who reside in the same city, who have a specific geographic region they support, and report to the same HR Director. Occasionally, they meet together with their leader to plan and budget for the year, yet their direct interactions with each other are infrequent and not necessarily work-driven. Customer service representatives within the same building who respond to inbound calls from customers and whose performance is measured and compensated individually are another example.

Virtual teams require greater flexibility from leaders and members due to the complexity and reliance differences. The key is to identify which factors are most influential and then put in place explicit work processes that clarify team goals, team member accountabilities, and ways to engage team members so that they are focused on accomplishing their tasks despite the distractions of virtual work. As the team's work progresses, these will likely need to be revisited and adapted periodically, but it's always best to begin with clarity.

Now that you understand the complexity and reliance of your team, how are these differences affecting your team? It is time to review the challenges Shonda is facing with respect to the complexity of her global virtual team.

What Are Shonda's Virtual Team Challenges?

Global virtual teams, like Shonda's are highly complex due to large differences in geography, time zones, culture and technology. Moreover, for teams like Shonda's, there is a high level of reliance or interdependence among team members. High reliance refers to the extent to which the individual work of one team member impacts the work of other members. For example, Shonda's team was counting on Liling and Hamad to collaborate on the strategy overview for that segment of the business development presentation. When that didn't happen, everyone was affected. Aisha had a different understanding of the priority of the financial projections. This also caused problems for everyone. High Complexity/High Reliance teams are the most difficult and challenging of all virtual teams.

Before we address Shonda's options for the immediate future (i.e. what she and the team can do now to get ready for their presentation to senior management on Monday), let's look first at some of their challenges and then what critical steps that, if completed, might have avoided her current dilemma.

Long-Distance Leadership Model™

We will address these challenges and potential solutions using the framework and steps in our Long-Distance Leadership Model. This model represents the prescribed stages and steps within each stage that, when followed, create a path that dramatically increases the chances for success.

The Long-Distance Leadership Model is diagnostic as well as prescriptive. If a team is struggling, the model can be applied to diagnose in which stage the difficulties lie and potential solutions for addressing them. It is interesting to note that difficulties teams experience in later stages of the model are usually influenced by steps in previous stages. For example, when there's a lack of engagement by one or more team members, it could be because the team neglected to discuss and create agreements for participation and building relationships. Let's look at the EMCA Foodservice team's challenges and what they could have done to avoid some of the problems they currently face. It is likely you'll see how each stage impacts the subsequent ones.

When assessing a virtual team's challenges and preparing a recommendation plan, it is important to answer three questions:

1) Which type of virtual team is being led with respect to complexity and reliance?

2) In which Long-Distance Leadership stage is the virtual team now? (Plan, Prepare, Produce or Results?)

3) Is the virtual team equipped to be in this stage?

- If **Yes**, proceed to check the predictors of high performance.
- If **No**, the virtual team should "Review, Adjust and Redirect" (**RAR**).
  - After RAR, the team should ensure all elements within initial stages of the Long-Distance Leadership Model are met before moving forward.

What is RAR?

Review, Adjust, and Redirect (RAR) is a stage in the model that serves as a reminder that, no matter how well planned, things on a virtual team are dynamic and even the best-laid plans may require a change. These sometimes become apparent when a team's lead or lag indicators suggest that things are not progressing as expected, when problems occur, or when there is a noticeable change in team member engagement or conflicts.

As mentioned previously, many virtual teams struggle to reach high performance levels, especially at first. A beneficial practice is to **Review** the status of your team at each stage as it moves to the next one. For instance, before a team moves into the Produce stage, it's a good idea to review if everyone has the same understanding of commitments made in the Team Operating Agreement. If not, spending some time adjusting and redirecting can avoid misunderstandings and problems later. In fact, when you detect problems in the **Produce** stage of the model (e.g. deadlines are being missed), a look back to the **Prepare** stage, may provide some insights to questions such as, "Are team members clear about the deadlines? Did we consider time differences or national holidays when we set the deadlines? Were the goals specific, measurable and time-bound?" This sort of review can provide insights as to what adjustments are needed to get things back on track.

Virtual team challenges are most apparent in the Produce and Results stages of the Long-Distance Leadership Model. You may recall from an earlier chapter, I mentioned lead and lag indicators as a way to track and assess individual and team performance. Lag indicators are the qualitative and quantitative results of team member behaviors and collaborations (relationships) which are lead indicators. The following table offers examples of both types of indicators and clues as to when things aren't going well and it's time to Review, Adjust and Redirect.

	Lead Indicators		Lag Indicators
Data Sources	**Individual Team Members**	**Team Member Relation- ships**	**Outputs/ Results**
• Leader Observa- tions • Project Plans • Stake- holder & Member Feedback • Meeting Behaviors • Status Reports • Team As- sessments	• Low en- gagement • Poor listen- ing • Inap- propriate behaviors • Stress responses • Skill gaps • Lack of availability • Slow re- sponses	• Conflicts with other mem- bers • Unwill- ing-ness to help others • Nega- tive com- ments • Low trust • Gossip about others	• Late/ missed deadlines • Poor qual- ity of work • Low pro- ductivity • Amount of rework

When Problems Arise

If leaders sense there are problems within the team, they should not hesitate to explore these further. It is far easier to coach and provide feedback to redirect ineffective team member behaviors (lead indicators) earlier than later. These are what I call "five-degree course adjustments." Too often, we hesitate to address issues hoping they will go away or take care of themselves. Unfortunately, this is generally not the case and a five-degree course adjustment left unattended, results in having to make a major correction or compromising results.

Issues that arise with individual team members are best addressed through one-on-one coaching conversations. Prior to the one-on-one, a leader should gather enough information from the data sources they have to provide clear examples of behaviors that were not effective. Ask for the team member's perspective and how he/she views the situation and gain a mutual understanding. When appropriate, engage the team member in creating an action plan to redirect their behaviors to have a more positive impact. Conclude the conversation by ensuring there is mutual understanding and agreement as to next steps and a clear time commitment for a follow-up conversation to assess progress.

For **differences or conflicts between two team members**, holding individual and joint coaching conversations may be necessary to fully understand and address the issues in order to either resolve them or create an action plan for further joint problem solving. Just as with individual issues, leaders should gather information prior to these conversations so that they can provide examples to illustrate the impacts of the conflict.

Carefully consider **lead or lag indicators of problems affecting the entire team**. Leaders should first do some self-reflection to consider their contribution to the issues. For relatively minor ones, it is often helpful for a team leader to raise the issues with the team as a whole and invite their input. Provide an opportunity for anonymous team member input as well as written or verbal feedback that identifies the provider. Recognize that some team members will hesitate to speak up in a team meeting in order to avoid perceived conflicts or embarrassment. In some cultures it is considered disrespectful for a team member to offer a viewpoint different from their leader or to speak about problems directly. Understanding and positively responding to cultural as well as individual differences among team members is key to trusting, productive relationships and solutions. **For issues that cannot be resolved by the leader or team members themselves**, it is often helpful to bring in a third party to provide coaching and facilitate a process that moves the team forward toward achieving high performance.

What's important to remember is that "anything that can go wrong with a face-to-face team can go wrong with a virtual team -only usually faster and less gracefully." Knowing the stages and components of the Long-Distance Leadership Model™ and the importance of addressing minor issues and problems before they become major, will make the journey to high virtual team performance faster and smoother.

Shonda's Virtual Team Assessment

Start with the following questions:

1) Which type of virtual team is being led with respect to complexity and reliance?

Based on our matrix, Shonda is leading a High Complexity/High Reliance team. Remember, the overall team performance is the sum total of both the members' and the leader's individual contributions. And, High Complexity/High Reliance teams are the most challenging to be a member of and to lead.

2) In which Long-Distance Leadership stage is the virtual team now? (Plan, Prepare, Produce or Results?)

Shonda's virtual team is in the Produce stage. We know this because they are meeting face-to-face to finalize a presentation based on prior research and individual team member efforts. In this stage, Shonda should focus on **ensuring high quality leader and member communication and maintaining high productivity and engagement**. The project will continue after the presentation so they are not yet at the Results stage.

3) Is the virtual team equipped to be in this stage?

Based on the breakdown in communication between some virtual members, Shonda as the virtual leader, and among all the members themselves, it is clear that this virtual team is not being successful in the Produce stage. This means the team should "Review, Adjust and Redirect" (**RAR**). Here are the steps to Review, Adjust and Redirect Shonda's virtual team:

Step 1: Review the Team Challenges

We start by creating a list of the challenges observed from the dialogue in Chapter 1:

1. Over the course of their work, **team members became confused** about the goals, priorities, and timelines of their deliverables.
2. Without training, Shonda and the team members were **unprepared to deal with**

the unique challenges of differences in time zones, geography, culture, technology.

3. Little thought or attention was given to **onboarding the team**. Without an initial face-to-face meeting, they missed their greatest opportunity to establish relationships, build trust, and create agreements for how to work together.

4. First language and cultural differences led to the **challenges of varying assumptions and behaviors** that affect decision making, role expectations, the need for details (context), participation and dealing with conflict.

5. With the stress on productivity and time pressures, Shonda's communications focused on accomplishing tasks. Building relationships, coaching, and adequately facilitating virtual team meetings **took a backseat to "getting the work done."**

6. Lead and lag performance indicators were not established so that Shonda and the team could **track and assess their progress and performance**. Had they done so, they might have detected problems earlier and been able to provide positive recognition to achieving milestones along the way.

Step 2: Adjust the Team's Approach to Challenges

A great way to adjust a team's approach to challenges is to prepare a table, list the challenges in one column and list potential recommendations in the next column:

Team Challenges	Recommendations
1. Over the course of their work, **team members became confused** about the goals, priorities, and timelines of their deliverables.	**PLAN** Before the launch of any virtual team, organizational leaders should answer the following questions: • **Drivers**—what organizational factors are driving the need for employees to work virtually? • **Obstacles**—what are the challenges to achieving the team's goals (e.g. multiple time zones, competing roles, access to information, multiple reporting relationships, etc)? • **Resources**—what resources are available to support mobile employees and virtual team members' work (e.g. budget, equipment, technology, etc.)? • **Articulate team purpose and vision**—what purpose and results (goals) are expected and how do they align with the organization's goals? • **Determine skills needed for the overall team**—beyond technical, what additional skills are needed for the team to be able to accomplish its goals? Developing answers for these and, perhaps other questions, sets up the team for success before it is even formed. If these are not clearly answered initially, they may need to be revisited to ensure that the team has what it needs to succeed.

Team Challenges	Recommendations
2. Without training, Shonda and the team members were **unprepared to deal with the unique challenges** of differences in time zones, geography, culture, technology. Consequently, conflicts arose.	**PREPARE** Once the necessary team leader and member skills have been identified: • Use assessments in the selection of individuals who have the behaviors and skills that contribute to effective virtual teams (visit LiterallyVirtually.comfor examples) • Where there are skill gaps, provide training that is specific to virtual teams.
3. Little thought or attention was given to **onboarding the team**. Without an initial face-to-face meeting, they missed their greatest opportunity to establish relationships, build trust, and create agreements for how to work together.	**PREPARE** If possible, onboard team members with a face-to-face meeting. During this meeting, set aside time to: • Reinforce members' understanding of the team's mission, vision and goals • Create a Team Operating Agreement that incorporates protocols for uses of technology, work procedures, sharing information and success measures • Discuss individual communication and recognition preferences, national cultures, and how the team will make decisions and address conflicts. If a face-to-face meeting is not possible, conduct a series of video-based onboarding sessions that focus team interaction on these topics.

Team Challenges	Recommendations
4. First language and cultural differences led to the **challenges of varying assumptions and behaviors** that affected decision making, role expectations, the need for details (context), participation and dealing with conflict.	**PREPARE** For global virtual teams, provide additional training on intercultural leadership, communications. and collaboration. Shonda's team experienced conflicts related to gender, communication styles, power, generational differences, risk avoidance, and individual versus group orientation. At least some of these conflicts could have been avoided and improved the team's efficiency by investing in training upfront and developing a team culture of openness and mutual support.
5. With the stress of productivity and time pressures, Shonda's communications focused on accomplishing tasks. Building relationships, coaching, and adequately facilitating virtual team meetings **took a backseat to "getting the work done."**	**PRODUCE** To ensure high quality leader and member communication, Shonda can do the following: • Conduct regular one-on-one leader/team member coaching conversations. Use this time to build relationships, address individual concerns and problems. Provide constructive feedback based on observations of team members' behaviors (lead indicators) and accomplishments (lag indicators). Ask for their feedback in return. • Invite team member suggestions for ways to improve team processes, procedures, and meetings. • Leverage technology such as polls, chats, breakout rooms to engage team members during meetings and reduce multi-tasking. • Invest time socializing and building relationships during meetings. Address any negative behaviors promptly.

Team Challenges	Recommendations
6. Lead and lag performance indicators were not established so that Shonda and the team could **track and assess their progress and performance**. Had they done so, they might have detected problems earlier and been able to provide positive recognition to achieving milestones along the way.	**PRODUCE** To maintain high productivity and engagement, Shonda can: • Identify the lag indicators (outputs/results) team members will be individually and collectively accountable for achieving. These may include productivity goals, milestone tasks, and standards for quality, service, and timeliness. Most, if not all, of these indicators can be quantitatively measured. • Define the lead indicators (behaviors) team member will apply to achieve their results. These include emotional intelligence behaviors such as self-awareness and management of emotions (e.g. calm under stress, sets personal goals, takes accountability for own actions) that contribute to positive, productive team member relationships. Lead indicators also include social awareness and relationship management skills such as listening, expressing empathy, coaching others, and showing respect and support of others. • Select the data sources that will be used to track lead and lag indicators. These may include project plans and status reports, stakeholder feedback, leader observations, and team member feedback. Use this information to coach and guide team members. • To maintain engagement during this stage, find ways to make the work enjoyable, make time to socialize and build relationships during team meetings, and celebrate milestone achievements, **RESULTS** To keep the team focused on results, Shonda can: • Remind team members of the team's purpose, vision and goals and how their progress brings them closer to achieving them. • Continue to acknowledge and celebrate milestones. • Provide progress reports to stakeholders and invite their feedback to be shared with the team. • Offer personalized recognition and reward as appropriate for positive behaviors and performance.

Step 3: Redirect the virtual team to the appropriate stage in the Long-Distance Leadership Model and remain vigilant for future challenges.

The recommendations for each of Shonda's team challenges point to the stage of the model where they should be addressed:

- **For Team Challenge #1:** if the goals, priorities, and timelines of the deliverables have changed, it may be necessary to discuss these with the key stakeholders and the impact these have on the team's ability to deliver. If they have not changed, the team should direct their efforts to the **Prepare** stage to create or revise their Team Operating Agreement and quickly move to **Produce.**
- **Team Challenges #2-4:** can also be addressed in the **Prepare** stage. These challenges are a result of a lack of adequate preparation and training of the team members for the unique aspects of virtual team work.
- **Team Challenges #5-6:** are for Shonda in particular. She will need to balance her focus on "accomplishing tasks" with building

relationships, coaching, and facilitating virtual team meetings that are both productive and engaging. These are steps in the **Produce** stage. As the team moves to producing **Results**, Shonda, working with her team members, can more accurately specify the lead and lag performance indicators they will use to track and assess their performance against their milestones and ultimately final results.

With these challenges addressed, this team can redirect their efforts to delivering timely **Results**.

Had Shonda and her team known how to handle some of the key differences between virtual and co-located teams, they likely would have avoided many of these challenges. How many of these challenges have you experienced? What can you do to address them now?

With a better grasp on the challenging areas for virtual teams, let's go back to the team meeting in progress to see how Shonda can reclaim control over the meeting and rectify the problem areas to allow the members to complete their project presentation.

CHAPTER 4

The Planning Meeting (Revisited)

Shonda is jarred back to reality as Vasili and Gustavo both stand up and start shouting at each other. She knew she had to do something fast to get things back on track. It was definitely time to **Review, Adjust and Redirect**. Shonda stood up, and calmly began to speak to get control of the meeting again.

SHONDA: If everyone could take a seat, I would appreciate it. I'd like to take a minute to pause and allow everyone to write down the issues they are having with completing their responsibilities with this project.

After a minute has elapsed, Shonda brings the team back to focus. She has written some bullet points on the chart at the front of the room.

SHONDA: As team leader, it is important for me to reiterate the purpose and vision for this team. I selected each of you based on your unique skills and abilities to create a dynamite business development plan to globally expand EMCA Foodservice's markets.

(Shonda directs the group's attention to the chart.)

SHONDA: (continues) I have listed each of your names here with your unique skill that you bring to this team. Now, I would like to create a shared vision with all of your input to fulfill our purpose.

It is something we should have established during our first meeting, I admit. However, it is not too late to accomplish this. Let's start by going around the room and I will read aloud your unique skill and each of you can share the single greatest issue you've had with collaborating with this virtual group We will start to my left with Gustavo...

(After completing this task, Shonda's chart appears as follows:)

	Unique Skill	Greatest Challenge
Gustavo	existing knowledge of business development and customer analytics of a potential emerging market (Brazil)	feels his contributions are not wanted (overshadowed by those with longer tenure)
Liling	international business savvy, can perceive what hurdles may exist in entering the Chinese market	feels that the team does not trust her strategy development due to her age
Jeff	scope out tasks, assignments and deliverables and to administer timelines	feels unnecessary to the group due to Shonda's micromanagement
Hamad	IT and foodservice expertise in a potential emerging market (Saudi Arabia)	feels he is left "out of the loop" for many differences due to time zone difference
Aisha	financial modeling, accuracy in predicting profit margins	feels she is not fully part of the team as the only contractor
Vasili	strong relationships with executive team (from tenure) - anticipates pushback that may be received	feels his views are considered "outdated" due to his age and tenure

Let's pause to look for any patterns here. What do you see in common among these virtual team members? Here's an initial list:

- Lack of trust in abilities
- Lack of engagement due to physical distance and large time differences
- Mixed understanding of clear purpose and group goals

Even one of these elements is enough to cause discord within a team, let alone a virtual team. If you were Shonda, how would you overcome these issues to get everyone back on track?

My suggestion is to address the issues and refocus our energy and direction. Creating clear agreements (#4 in the Long-Distance Leadership Model in the Prepare stage) can combat future issues from reoccurring and keep the team on track. At this stage, if the project is to be successful, they must now come together, work through their differences and fulfill their commitment to assemble their report and deliver a presentation for the senior leaders. Their collective success depends on each member both doing their individual parts and extra to work together to make this happen. Shonda clarified the need for high-quality leader-to-member and member-to-member communication (#5 in the Long-Distance Leadership Model in the Produce stage).

Here is a sample of the agreed-upon Communication and Collaboration Protocols:

We can ensure a positive communication and collaboration experience by:

- Requiring full participation during meetings - no multitasking
- Recording virtual conferences (phone and/or video) to ensure all members have access to the information
- Rotating meeting times and using visual technology to support engagement

Additional Rules of Engagement:

- All team member requests will be addressed within 1 business day (24 hours within time of receipt) and answered within 2 business days (unless otherwise indicated)
- No team meetings will be held during religious days of the week (unless all team members agree on that date)
- The team website will be used for shared document and email for one-on-one communications; all team decisions will be made during live conferences
- In the event of a conflict or disagreement, team members should first take steps to resolve it; Shonda will serve as the mediator, if necessary.

Finally, Shonda asked each member to voice their opinion on which countries should be the primary and secondary markets for the presentation.

Though some members were disappointed at the opinions voiced by others, they knew that if they were not united now, they would miss a major milestone expected by the senior leaders.

Once the majority spoke and highlighted China and Greece as the primary markets and Brazil and Saudi Arabia as the secondary markets, Shonda took an anonymous poll to determine if there was full team member support to the prioritization. When the ballots were tallied, all had agreed. She then went on to thank the team members and ask them to pledge their commitment to work together over the next two days so that they were fully prepared for Monday's presentation.

Lessons Learned

Shonda went on to explain, that she now understood how she and other team members did not fully recognize the many challenges associated with remote work and virtual teams, especially within a global virtual team. As she reflected, she realized she had missed the signs that indicated there were problems team members were having in sharing information, collaborating and communicating. She now saw how team member differences in generations, culture, reporting relationships and the need for details had complicated their already complex assignments.

For the remainder of the meeting (keeping in mind the new Communication and Collaboration Protocols), the team easily came to the following decisions:

- The team would work into the evening to-day (Friday) and as much as needed on Saturday. Hamad would be excused for prayer time. They would not to work on Sunday morning so that all team members had time for personal activities. If necessary, they would reassemble Sunday afternoon to prepare for their presentation.

- Since China and Greece are the primary markets, Liling, Hamad and Vasili would work together to clarify and finalize the strategies for each one and identify synergies. When finished, Gustavo would replace Vasili as they moved to the secondary market priorities of Brazil and Saudi Arabia. Shonda and Aisha would review the strategies and add the financial components. Based on the strategies, Jeff can scope the major components and milestones for each market followed by a review from the whole team.

- Shonda and Jeff would outline the key presentation components and hand the outline to Liling, Vasili, and Gustavo who would prepare the visuals and their speaking parts to support Shonda and Jeff's input.

- Once the plan was in place, the entire team would assemble virtually (if meeting on Sunday) or in-person (early Monday morning) for presentation rehearsal and feedback.

The team now has a game plan. But, does it work?

Over the weekend, some interesting things happened as Shonda and her team worked together. United by a clear sense of purpose, goals, and roles, each member seemed to gain energy and enthusiasm as they focused on the tasks in front of them.

As Hamad and Liling worked jointly on strategy, Hamad became more open to Liling's expertise and showed more respect for her ideas. Liling came to understand why this was challenging for Hamad given the different roles between men and women in his culture. As they worked with Vasili and Gustavo, all of them realized how the business development strategies would have to be customized for the unique customer expectations in each country if they were going to be successful.

Once Aisha understood the priority of markets, she went to work forecasting the financials. She came to understand that she needed to raise her voice and show more confidence when she shared her projections with the team. When she did, team members showed renewed respect back.

Of course, everything did not go off without a hitch. Tension still remained between Shonda and Jeff. From her perspective, he seemed to be undermining her leadership by continually interjecting how he thought things should be done instead of following her lead. Jeff confided to Vasili that he believed Shonda was too demanding and that the main reason she was pushing the team was because she was focused on her likely promotion when this project was finished. After, Vasili shared this feedback with Shonda, he suggested that they may consider chatting with each other directly, and he would be happy to serve as a moderator. Once Shonda and Jeff met with Vasili offering to be a neutral third-party, Shonda agreed to adjust her management approach with the overall team to prove that she trusted their contributions. In exchange, Jeff was willing to follow Shonda's lead without questioning her process.

In the end, the presentation went off smoothly and their proposal was accepted by upper management. Shonda did receive a promotion to upper management, thanks to her leadership of a successful project. When she spoke with Karl, her leader about the promotion, she shared some of the key leadership lessons she had learned--sometimes the hard way. When Karl asked her what was the most important lesson she learned, Shonda replied, "There are many opportunities to leverage the power of the remote workforce, including virtual teams. But there are significant differences in engaging team members and creating high performance. If our organization and others don't address these differences and prepare their leaders and team members, we risk compromising what we are capable of achieving. If we are proactive and prepare well, we can achieve many great things. "

Weeks later, Shonda recommended that Aisha be brought on as a full-time employee and that Jeff be considered for a supervisor role within his department. By working on a virtual team with these individuals, she had an opportunity to view their leadership abilities and establish a strong case to promote these high performers within the organization.

Moving Forward

Shonda and her team are not unlike you and me. We all have our challenges. We all wish things were easier. But is through these challenges that we grow in our skills and our wisdom. I invite you to take what you have learned from Shonda and her team and apply it to your own virtual work experiences. As Mark Twain once said, "What gets us into trouble is not what we don't know, it's what we know for sure that just ain't so." Remain open to the possibilities and other's perspectives. If you apply the tools and techniques shared in this book, I am confident you, too, will literally, virtually change the world for the better.

Afterword

I remember a moment some time ago as I was driving one of my sons across town to run an errand when I received a call from a client in Saudi Arabia. After helping to talk through the issue the individual had and providing some direction, my son asked me how often I get calls from other countries. That moment caused me to reflect on the fact that I had just had a long call with a partner in China that morning, a call coordinating an update on our firm's assessment center with my team of programmers in Wisconsin, Miami, Chicago, and Connecticut, and finally this recent call from the Middle East. All this was being conducted from my home office in Washington state and it was still early in the afternoon. We truly live in a global and virtual world where the boundaries of interaction and are endless.

I am a member of a virtual team running a leadership development consulting firm. I also lead other virtual teams within the firm, as well as coach/train others in the skillset. From this perspective, I find *Literally Virtually* an invaluable resource that Lee Johnsen has provided. It is a salient reminder of the critical presence of virtual teams now and the explosion of growth they will see in the coming years as the global markets continue to grow, catalyzed by technological advances.

The success of organizations will hinge on the ability to embrace, leverage, build, and maintain virtual teams. In *Literally Virtually*, Johnsen has given us sound, practical suggestions to build a high performing virtual team. What I appreciate most is that he doesn't try to sugar coat the challenges of performing in a virtual team, but rather provides a framework, model, steps, and tools to increase the likelihood of your virtual team's success!

Obviously, the Long-Distance Leadership Model™ is at the core of this message, but I find the EQ component to be the most challenging as I am coaching leaders. Johnsen highlights the need to build trust, use clear, explicit communications, and coach with respect to cultural differences.

I recall recently working with an Executive Leadership Team where there was a member of the team who resided in the South, while the others resided in the East Coast. The individual was the new member of the group and was struggling to form a connection with the others, as well as feel like he was a good "fit" on the team. The steps Johnsen outlines made all the difference for the individual and the overall success of the team.

First, the team needed to focus on building trust with each other. This meant that trust was needed among each and every member of the team, not just the ones who worked on the same office floor. Consequently, a face to face team meeting was coordinated where he flew up to join the team in an exercise to share about their personal interests and backgrounds. The first half of the meeting had nothing to do with the execution of their daily work objectives. It was simply learning about each person's story.

Secondly, each member of the team was engaged to create and define a Team Operating Agreement to clarify expectations and rules for team engagement. Included in this agreement were the expectations on the method and frequency of communication to help make sure all team members felt included and aware of information critical to the success of the organization as well as a clear expectations to treat team members with respect.

With a more personal connection among all team members and a clear set of operating principles, the subsequent team meetings and interactions allowed for growth in all areas of the organization over the next year.

Furthermore, there are several assessments and checklists included in *Literally Virtually* to help establish a baseline of expectation and performance as well as identify areas of strength and deficiency. I have found that these types of resources to be tremendously helpful because they help the team leader recognize the unique needs of their team. No two virtual teams are the same and sometimes it can be hard to know where to focus as a leader.

The Virtual Team Assessment will provide the data necessary to guide you as the leader on that journey with concrete next steps. For example, being able to identify if the current difficulties of a team are due to relationship/trust issues, project management deficits, cultural issues, or communication problems will then allow the leader to know where the next steps should be.

Once a leader has identified the target areas, then they can turn to the respective chapter in *Literally Virtually* for added tips and suggestions on ways to shore-up that attribute of the team.

As the reader of this book, I applaud your desire to improve your virtual team leadership. I believe that my words have demonstrated how much I endorse and support the principles Johnsen has shared here.

Yet, I also want to provide another suggestion I learned from my father, John Parker Stewart.

He has taught me Leadership Gems since I was a young boy. One that has always stood out to me is the concept of ownership versus "rentership".

From a team building perspective, I believe it is essential to be as inclusive as possible in the team building process. Allow your team members to be a part of the team improvement and development process. Gather their ideas and suggestions. Solicit their input. Ask about their personal experiences. Help them feel not just as a renter in the group but as true owners in the team of ideas, tasks, processes, and accomplishments.

Even though geography may separate you as a team, by using the tools in *Literally Virtually* you can turn the virtual workspace to your advantage and lead a team of success!

Peter K. Stewart, PhD
Managing Director, Stewart Leadership
www.stewartleadership.com

Acknowledgements

There are many who have influenced this book—some by their presence and others by their spirit. I regret there is no way to acknowledge them all, but I want to thank a few who have been particularly helpful:

My dear colleague and editor, Lauren Young, who, without her kind persistence and encouragement, this book would not have been written;

My friend and colleague, Donna Dennis who has been a learning partner in understanding and teaching others about the challenges and opportunities of the virtual workforce; and

My associate, Jacob Bawolek, for his positive words and fresh perspectives.

I am deeply grateful to my ancestors and family and friends for their support and who encouraged me along this path.

Finally, I am grateful to my friend and spouse, Rex for his patience, encouragement, and confidence.

Appendix

Footnotes

1. Briggs, J. (2014, July 14). *RW3 Culture Wizard Unveils Biennial Survey Results for Effective Virtual Teaming*. CultureWizard by RW3, LLC. Retrieved from http://www.rw-3.com/blog/2014/07/rw3-culturewizard-unveils-biennial-survey-results-for-effective-virtual-teaming

2. Grenier, R., & Metes, G. (1995). *Going Virtual: Moving Your Organization Into the 21st Century*. Upper Saddle River, NJ: Prentice Hall PTR.

3. Dennis, D. (2014) *The New Dominance of Virtual Team and Leaders*. Business Research Consortium. Retrieved from http://www.leadership-solutions.info/BRC.html

4. *Successfully Transitioning to a Virtual Organization: Challenges, Impact and Technology*. (First Quarter 2010). SHRM Research Quarterly. Society for Human Resource Management.

5. Dennis, D. (2014) *The New Dominance of Virtual Team and Leaders*. Business Research Consortium. Retrieved from http://www.leadership-solutions.info/BRC.html

6. Bradberry, T., Greaves, J. and Lencioni, P. (2009). *Emotional Intelligence 2.0*. TalentSmart.

7. Bean, S. (2015, November 15) *Remote workers endure poor communications and working practices*. Workplace

Insight. Retrieved from http://workplaceinsight.net/
remote-workers-endure-poor-communications-and-
working-practices

8. Mehrabian, A. (1980). Silent Messages: Implicit
Communication of Emotions and Attitudes. Belmont,
CA: Wadsworth Publishing Company.

9. Brandon, J. (2017, April 17). *The Surprising Reason
Millennials Check Their Phones 150 Times a Day.* Inc.
com. Retrieved from http://www.inc.com/john-
brandon/science-says-this-is-the-reason-millennials-
check-their-phones-150-times-per-day.html

10. Brack, J. and Kelly, K. (2012). *Maximizing Millennials
in the Workplace.* UNC Executive Development.
Retrieved from http://www.kenan-flagler.unc.edu/
executive-development/custom-programs/~/media/
DF1C11C056874DDA8097271A1ED48662.ashx

11. Husman, R.C., Lahiff, J.M., & Penrose, J. M. (1988).
Business Communication Strategies and Skills. Chicago:
Dryden Press.

12. Mann, A. and Harter, J. (2016, January 7).*The
Worldwide Employee Engagement Crisis.* Gallup
Business Journal. Retrieved from http://news.gallup.
com/businessjournal/188033/worldwide-employee-
engagement-crisis.aspx

13. Corbin, J. (2017, March 7). The Gallup 2017 Employee
Engagement Report is Out: And the Results...Nothing
has Changed. LinkedIn. Retrieved from http://
www.linkedin.com/pulse/gallup-2017-employee-
engagement-report-out-results-nothing-corbin

14. *Remote Workers Log More Hours and Are Slightly More
Engaged.* (2013, July 12). Gallup Business Journal.
Retrieved from http://news.gallup.com/opinion/
gallup/170669/remote-workers-log-hours-slightly-
engaged.aspx

15. O'Brien, M. (2011, May 24). *Generational Differences in
Recognition and Rewards.* Human Resources Executive
Online. Retrieved from http://www.hreonline.com/
HRE/view/story.jhtml?id=533338164

16. Ferrazzi, K. (December 2014). *Getting Virtual Teams Right*. Harvard Business Review. Retrieved from http://hbr.org/2014/12/getting-virtual-teams-right

17. Example websites include: http://www.drbobnelson.com/site/ideas, www.pmi.org/learning/library/successful-motivational-techniques-virtual-teams-8161 and http://blog.hubstaff.com/motivating-employees-who-work-remotely

18. Schell, A. (2016, April 26). *Trends in Virtual Teams*. CultureWizard by RW3, LLC. Retrieved from http://www.rw-3.com/blog/trends-in-global-virtual-teams

19. Briggs, J. (2014, July 14). *RW3 Culture Wizard Unveils Biennial Survey Results for Effective Virtual Teaming*. CultureWizard by RW3. Retrieved from http://www.rw-3.com/blog/2014/07/rw3-culturewizard-unveils-biennial-survey-results-for-effective-virtual-teaming

20. Dennis, D. (2014) *The New Dominance of Virtual Team and Leaders*. Business Research Consortium. Retrieved from http://www.leadership-solutions.info/BRC.html

21. *State of the American Workplace*. (2016). Gallup News. Retrieved from http://news.gallup.com/reports/199961/state-american-workplace-report-2016.aspx

Discussion Questions

Chapter 1

1. Everyone on Shonda's team has expert technical skills and is a strong performer in her/his field. What other skills do you think it would take them to be successful virtual team members?

2. Shonda and her team members had prepared for their face-to-face meeting. An agenda was provided, and each member was given specific assignments, yet the meeting did not go well. What do you think went wrong? What could they have done differently to make their first face-to-face meeting successful?

3. What do you think are the differences (culture, generation, gender, work function, etc.) among the team members? How did these differences affect their interactions? If you are part of a virtual team, what differences do you notice among team members? How do they affect interactions?

4. What could Shonda's boss, Karl Norris, have done to support the team up to this point?

Chapter 2

1. If you are a part of a virtual team, how clearly and consistently could the team members explain the team's purpose and vision? What effect do these have on the team when everyone is aligned behind them? What if they are not clearly understood or supported?

2. What do you see as the key differences between being a member of a virtual team compared to one whose members are all in one location? How do these differences affect the team's performance?

3. Does your team have a Team Operating Agreement? If not, could the team benefit from creating one?

4. How would you rate the level of trust (1 = low; 5 = high) among your team members? What are the consequences?

5. How would you rate the effectiveness of your virtual team meetings? (1 = low; 5 = high) What are the consequences?

6. Of the Eight Predictors of High Performance, which two are strengths of your team? Which two need improvement?

Chapter 3

1. What are the top challenges of your virtual team? What ideas do you have to address these challenges?
2. Does your team have active support from key stakeholders? If not, how could you further engage them?
3. In which of the Complexity and Reliance quadrants is your team?
(High Complexity/Low Reliance, High Complexity/High Reliance,
Low Complexity/High Reliance, Low Complexity/Low Reliance). How do these factors affect the team's productivity and relationships?
4. How can you build on the strengths of your team members to achieve higher levels of performance and trusting relationships?
5. In which Stage(s) and Steps of the Long-Distance Leadership Model is your team? Are things going well? If not, is now a time to Review, Adjust, and Redirect? If not now, when?

Chapter 4

1. Upon review, Shonda and her team have begun to adjust and redirect the way in which they work together. They applied some of the strategies and methods outlined in the

Long-Distance Leadership Model. What else do they need to do to reach high virtual team performance?

2. After Shonda's team completes this project, what advice do you think the team could share with others in their organization about being a successful virtual team member?

3. What lessons from Shonda's team can you apply? If your team members are all located in one country how would that affect their work and relationships?

4. What lessons learned could be applied to leaders of team members who telecommute or work remotely and have relatively little reliance on other members? Their primary focus is on their individual assignments and relationship with their manager.

5. What are the first three actions you commit to taking to be a more effective virtual team leader or member?

About Lee Johnsen

Lee S. Johnsen, CPT, CPLP, SPHR, is an international leader in the fields of virtual team management, leadership development, and performance improvement. Lee brings his unique expertise to coaching and consulting with executives and leaders. He is an expert at helping teams and their leaders navigate the challenges and opportunities of the virtual workforce—domestically and globally.

Lee is Principal and Founder of Partners in Development (PID). He has nearly 30 years' experience in successfully guiding organizations to improve productivity and develop leaders. He has worked with clients from industries including oil and gas, financial services, government, third-party logistics, private education, health care, insurance, and nonprofits. In 2014, he spent five months developing young leaders in Saudi Arabia.

A results-oriented professional, focused on helping organizations achieve excellence, he is a known leader in performance improvement. Lee's areas of expertise encompass, executive coaching, strategic planning, leadership and management development training, employee engagement, and emotional intelligence. His career has included officer and management positions in Fortune 500 corporations as well as government agencies.

Lee has the international distinction of being one of only a few who is credentialed by three international human resources organizations— Association for Talent Development (ATD), International Society for Performance Improvement (ISPI), and Society for Human Resource Management (SHRM). He is a published author of several articles and co-authored the book *Real World Teambuilding Strategies That Work* (Insight Publishing).

Audiences describe Lee's speaking style as down-to-earth, humorous, and insightful. He is rated as one of the top leadership speakers for the American Management Association. One participant summarized it this way, "Lee, I have to tell you that this has been the best seminar experience in my career. That is entirely thanks to you. Your expertise and delivery were tremendous. THANK YOU."

Lee and his spouse reside in Madison, Wisconsin where they enjoy many outdoor activities with friends and family.

CPSIA information can be obtained
at www.ICGtesting.com
Printed in the USA
LVHW091758210420
654190LV00004B/1248